KETO DIET COOKBOOK FOR WOMEN AFTER 50

THE ULTIMATE KETOGENIC GUIDE WITH 200 AMAZING RECIPES TO BETTER FACE MENOPAUSE AND LOSE WEIGHT, BOOST YOUR ENERGY, AND REGAIN YOUR VITALITY

Kety Womack

Copyright - 2020 -

All rights reserved.

The content contained within this book may not be reproduced, duplicated or transmitted without direct written permission from the author or the publisher.

Under no circumstances will any blame or legal responsibility be held against the publisher, or author, for any damages, reparation, or monetary loss due to the information contained within this book. Either directly or indirectly.

Legal Notice:

This book is copyright protected. This book is only for personal use. You cannot amend, distribute, sell, use, quote or paraphrase any part, or the content within this book, without the consent of the author or publisher.

Disclaimer Notice:

Please note the information contained within this document is for educational and entertainment purposes only. All effort has been executed to present accurate, up to date, and reliable, complete information. No warranties of any kind are declared or implied. Readers acknowledge that the author is not engaging in the rendering of legal, financial, medical or professional advice. The content within this book has been derived from various sources. Please consult a licensed professional before attempting any techniques outlined in this book.

By reading this document, the reader agrees that under no circumstances is the author responsible for any losses, direct or indirect, which are incurred as a result of the use of information contained within this document, including, but not limited to, - errors, omissions, or inaccuracies.

TABLE OF CONTENTS

INTRODUCTION   10

1. THE KETOGENIC DIET   12

2. CHALLENGES SENIORS OVER 50 FACES DURING THE KETO DIET AND HOW TO AVOID THEM   14

3. FOODS ALLOWED IN THE KETO DIET   18

4. WHAT DOES THE KETOGENIC DIET MEAN TO WOMEN AFTER 50?   22

5. HOW THE KETOGENIC DIET HELPS WITH THE SIGN AND SYMPTOMS OF AGEING AND MENOPAUSE   26

6. BREAKFAST RECIPES   28

1. KETO-FLU COMBAT SMOOTHIE   29
2. STRAWBERRIES AND CREAM SMOOTHIE   30
3. NO-BAKE KETO POWER BARS   31
4. BACON CHEESEBURGER WAFFLES   32
5. KETO BREAKFAST CHEESECAKE   33
6. BREAKFAST ROLL-UPS   34
7. BASIC OPIE ROLLS   35
8. CREAM CHEESE PANCAKE   36
9. BLUEBERRY COCONUT PORRIDGE   37
10. CAULIFLOWER HASH BROWNS   38
11. KETO ROLLS   39
12. NUT GRANOLA & SMOOTHIE BOWL   40
13. BACON AND EGG QUESADILLAS   41
14. SPICY EGG MUFFINS WITH BACON & CHEESE   42
15. DARK CHOCOLATE SMOOTHIE   43
16. FIVE GREENS SMOOTHIE   44

17. ALMOND WAFFLES WITH CINNAMON CREAM — 45
18. DELICIOUS POACHED EGGS — 46
19. KETO BREAKFAST BOWL — 47
20. YUMMY EGGS AND SAUSAGES — 48
21. BREAKFAST SCRAMBLED EGGS — 49
22. DELICIOUS FRITTATA — 50
23. SMOKED SALMON BREAKFAST — 51
24. FETA AND ASPARAGUS DELIGHT — 52
25. SPECIAL BREAKFAST EGGS — 53
26. EGGS BAKED IN AVOCADOS — 54
27. SHRIMP AND BACON BREAKFAST — 55

7. LUNCH RECIPES — 56

28. HOT BUFFALO WINGS — 57
29. TROUT AND CHILI NUTS — 58
30. AVOCADO AND KALE EGGS — 59
31. BACON AND CHEESE FRITTATA — 60
32. HAM & EGG BROCCOLI BAKE — 61
33. CHICKEN, BACON, AND AVOCADO CLOUD SANDWICHES — 62
34. ROASTED LEMON CHICKEN SANDWICH — 63
35. KETO-FRIENDLY SKILLET PEPPERONI PIZZA — 64
36. PESTO SHRIMP WITH ZUCCHINI NOODLES — 65
37. CHICKEN SOUP — 66
38. CHICKEN AVOCADO SALAD — 67
39. EASY MEATBALLS — 68
40. CHICKEN CASSEROLE — 69
41. LEMON BAKED SALMON — 70
42. CAULIFLOWER MASH — 71
43. BAKED SALMON — 72
44. TUNA PATTIES — 73
45. GRILLED MAHI WITH LEMON BUTTER SAUCE — 74
46. SHRIMP SCAMPI — 75

47. ITALIAN SAUSAGE STACKS	76
48. SMOKED SALMON ROLLS WITH DILL CREAM CHEESE	77
49. SPINACH CHICKEN CHEESY BAKE	78
50. CILANTRO CHICKEN BREASTS WITH MAYO-AVOCADO SAUCE	79
51. CHICKEN DRUMSTICKS IN TOMATO SAUCE	80
52. ROASTED CHICKEN BREASTS WITH CAPERS	81
53. SWEET GARLIC CHICKEN SKEWERS	82
54. CHICKEN IN WHITE WINE SAUCE	83
55. STUFFED CHICKEN BREASTS WITH CUCUMBER NOODLE SALAD	84
56. PARMESAN WINGS WITH YOGURT SAUCE	85
57. CREAMY STUFFED CHICKEN WITH PARMA HAM	86
58. CHICKEN CAULIFLOWER BAKE	87
8. DINNER RECIPES	**88**
59. TURMERIC CHICKEN AND CABBAGE SALAD WITH LEMON AND HONEY	89
60. EGG-CRUST PIZZA	90
61. CHICKEN BROCCOLI DINNER	91
62. CHICKEN BACON BURGER	92
63. BASIL CHICKEN SAUTÉ	93
64. SLOW COOKER JERK CHICKEN	94
65. PULLED BUFFALO CHICKEN SALAD WITH BLUE CHEESE	95
66. LAMB BURGERS WITH TZATZIKI	96
67. LAMB SLIDERS	97
68. NO-PASTRY BEEF WELLINGTON	98
69. LAMB SOUVLAKI	99
70. LAMB SAAGWALA	100
71. ROGAN JOSH	101
72. TILAPIA WITH PARMESAN BARK	102
73. BLACKENED FISH TACOS WITH SLAW	103
74. MOZZARELLA FISH	104
75. CRAB CASSEROLE	105

76. SALMON SKEWERS IN CURED HAM	106
77. FISH CASSEROLE WITH CREAM CHEESE SAUCE	107
78. BACON AND JALAPENO WRAPPED SHRIMP	108
79. CRISPY FISH STICK	109
80. PROSCIUTTO-WRAPPED COD	110
81. COCONUT MAHI-MAHI NUGGETS	111
82. GARLIC & GINGER CHICKEN WITH PEANUT SAUCE	112
83. EASY CHICKEN CHILI	113
84. EGGPLANT & TOMATO BRAISED CHICKEN THIGHS	114
85. LEMON-GARLIC CHICKEN SKEWERS	115
86. SWEET CHILI GRILLED CHICKEN	116
87. CHICKEN & SQUASH TRAYBAKE	117
9. VEGETABLES RECIPES	**118**
88. FRIED GARLIC BACON AND BOK CHOY BROTH	119
89. JICAMA FRIES	120
90. CURRY SPICED ALMONDS	121
91. SALTED KALE CHIPS	122
92. TOASTED PUMPKIN SEEDS	123
93. CAULIFLOWER CHEESE DIP	124
94. BUTTER GREEN PEAS	125
95. LEMON ASPARAGUS	126
96. LIME GREEN BEANS	127
97. CHEESE ASPARAGUS	128
98. CREAMY BROCCOLI	129
99. GARLIC EGGPLANT	130
100. COCONUT BRUSSELS SPROUTS	131
101. CAULIFLOWER PILAF WITH HAZELNUTS	132
102. CAULIFLOWER AND TURMERIC MASH	133
103. SPINACH AND OLIVES MIX	134
104. RED CABBAGE AND WALNUTS	135
105. PAPRIKA BOK CHOY	136

106. ZUCCHINI MIX	137
107. ZUCCHINI AND SPRING ONIONS	138
108. CREAMY PORTOBELLO MIX	139
109. EGGPLANT MASH	140
110. CHEDDAR ARTICHOKE	141
111. SQUASH AND ZUCCHINIS	142
112. DILL LEEKS	143
113. VEGETABLE LASAGNA	144
10. POULTRY AND EGGS RECIPES	**146**
114. TASTY CHICKEN WITH BRUSSELS SPROUTS	147
115. CHAFFLES WITH SCRAMBLED EGGS	148
116. AROMATIC JALAPENO WINGS	149
117. BARBEQUE CHICKEN WINGS	150
118. SAUCY DUCK	151
119. CHICKEN ROUX GUMBO	152
120. CIDER-BRAISED CHICKEN	153
121. CHUNKY CHICKEN SALSA	154
122. DIJON CHICKEN	155
123. CHICKEN THIGHS WITH VEGETABLES	156
124. CHICKEN DIPPED IN TOMATILLO SAUCE	157
125. CHICKEN WITH LEMON PARSLEY BUTTER	158
126. PAPRIKA CHICKEN	159
127. ROTISSERIE CHICKEN	160
128. CROCKPOT CHICKEN ADOBO	161
129. CHICKEN GINGER CURRY	162
130. THAI CHICKEN CURRY	163
11. MEAT RECIPES	**164**
131. BEEF, PEPPER, AND GREEN BEANS STIR-FRY	165
132. GARLIC STEAKS WITH ROSEMARY	166
133. BALSAMIC PORK TENDERLOIN	167
134. CARNITAS	168

135. CHILE VERDE	169
136. CHIMICHURRI PORK ROAST	170
137. GINGER & LIME PORK	171
138. KALUA PORK & CABBAGE	172
139. PORK HOCK	173
140. PULLED PORK	174
141. SPICY PORK CHOPS	175
142. LAMB BARBACOA	176
143. LAMB WITH MINT & GREEN BEANS	177
144. TARRAGON LAMB SHANK & BEANS	178
145. TASTY & EASY LAMB	179
12. SEAFOOD RECIPES	**180**
146. BACON-WRAPPED MAHI-MAHI	181
147. GARLIC BUTTER SALMON	182
148. SALMON WITH GREEN BEANS	183
149. SALMON SHEET PAN	184
150. BACON-WRAPPED SALMON	185
151. STIR-FRY TUNA WITH VEGETABLES	186
152. CHILI-GLAZED SALMON	187
153. CARDAMOM SALMON	188
154. CREAMY TUNA, SPINACH, AND EGGS PLATES	189
155. TUNA AND AVOCADO	190
156. BAKED FISH WITH FETA AND TOMATO	191
13. SNACK RECIPES	**192**
157. BLUEBERRY SCONES	193
158. HOMEMADE GRAHAM CRACKERS	194
159. BUFFALO CHICKEN SAUSAGE BALLS	195
160. BRUSSELS SPROUTS CHIPS	196
161. KETO CHOCOLATE MOUSSE	197
162. KETO BERRY MOUSSE	198
163. PEANUT BUTTER MOUSSE	199

164. COOKIE ICE CREAM	200
165. MOCHA ICE CREAM	201
166. RASPBERRY CREAM FAT BOMBS	202
167. CAULIFLOWER TARTAR BREAD	203
168. BUTTERY SKILLET FLATBREAD	204
169. FLUFFY BITES	205
170. COCONUT FUDGE	206
171. NUTMEG NOUGAT	207
172. SWEET ALMOND BITES	208
173. STRAWBERRY CHEESECAKE MINIS	209
174. COCOA BROWNIES	210
175. CHOCOLATE ORANGE BITES	211
176. ROASTED CAULIFLOWER WITH PROSCIUTTO, CAPERS, AND ALMONDS	212
177. BUTTERY SLOW-COOKER MUSHROOMS	213
178. BAKED ZUCCHINI GRATIN	214
179. ROASTED RADISHES WITH BROWN BUTTER SAUCE	215
180. PARMESAN AND PORK RIND GREEN BEANS	216
181. PESTO CAULIFLOWER STEAKS	217
182. TOMATO, AVOCADO, AND CUCUMBER SALAD	218
183. CRUNCHY PORK RIND ZUCCHINI STICKS	219
184. CHEESE CHIPS AND GUACAMOLE	220
185. CAULIFLOWER "POTATO" SALAD	221
186. LOADED CAULIFLOWER MASHED "POTATOES"	222
187. KETO BREAD	223
188. DEVILED EGGS	224
189. CHICKEN-PECAN SALAD CUCUMBER BITES	225
190. BUFFALO CHICKEN DIP	226
191. ROASTED BRUSSELS SPROUTS WITH BACON	227
192. SALAMI, PEPPERONCINI, AND CREAM CHEESE PINWHEELS	228
193. CAULIFLOWER STEAKS WITH BACON AND BLUE CHEESE	229

194. BACON-WRAPPED JALAPEÑOS — 230
195. CREAMY BROCCOLI-BACON SALAD — 231

14. DESSERTS RECIPES — 232

196. SOUTHERN APPLE PIE — 233
197. CHEESE BERRY PIE — 234
198. LEMON CHEESECAKE — 235
199. NO-GUILT CHOCOLATE CAKE — 236
200. THE BEST COOKIES — 237
201. SALTY CARAMEL CAKE — 238
202. LUSCIOUS RED VELVET CAKE — 239
203. SOUTHERN PECAN PIE — 240
204. CHIA SEED CRACKERS — 241
205. CHEESY BISCUITS — 242
206. KETO COCONUT FLAKE BALLS — 243
207. TOFU NUGGETS WITH CILANTRO DIP — 244
208. KETO CHOCOLATE GREEK YOGHURT COOKIES — 245
209. CHOCOLATE DIPPED CANDIED BACON — 246
210. TROPICAL COCONUT BALLS — 247
211. CHIA PEANUT BUTTER BITES — 248
212. ALMOND SESAME CRACKERS — 249

CONCLUSION — 250

INTRODUCTION

The ketogenic diet has been highly praised for the benefits of weight loss. This high-fat, low-carb diet is extremely healthy overall. It really makes your body burn fat, like a talking machine. Public figures appreciate it too. But the question is, how does ketosis enhance weight loss? The following is a detailed picture of the ketosis and weight loss process.

Dr. Mark Sissenwine is a professor at the Translational Medicine Research Institute and the Center for Obesity and Metabolic Syndrome. He is also an assistant professor of medicine. Dr. Sissenwine explains that this diet was the first diet which was meant for obesity," or Ketogenesis, if you will." On this diet, the body goes into a state of ketosis. He said. "This state of ketosis is what increases the number of calories your body burns, compared to the diet."

Ketosis may cause inflammation in the body, he explains. But it is not so bad. It is not bad for your body's performance and health. Dr. Sissenwine says, "Levels of ketosis increase when you reduce the number of carbohydrates you consume. As your low-carb intake increases, the body will need to find another source of fuel to use. It will switch to the fat it previously accumulated and it will begin to burn. The increase in ketosis is different for every person, depending on his exact weight and calorie intake. But it is a good thing to consider when consuming this diet."

As the body begins to burn fat cells, it can make you feel muscles for a short time. Interestingly, you can lose weight and gain muscle mass at the same time. Dr. Sissenwine says, "Your body has these amazing muscles that can pull on certain strings. Different from a puppeteer, you have to eat enough calories for the strings to work. So you want to eat what you want to eat. A typical menu for a ketogenic diet is high in fat, medium in protein and low in carbohydrates. Dr. Sissenwine says this diet is the best one for you.

The process of ketosis makes the body conserve the food you eat in your body. This makes your body work well during the day. It makes your brain function better. You get better health. You lose weight and most importantly, you lose fat in the weight loss. This diet is good to adopt. You would get a healthier body with faster weight loss. It will leave you in better shape.

We wish to thank Dr. Sissenwine for the wonderful information as a whole, but we would like to point out that this is not a cinch fast diet. This diet requires a significant amount of commitment and hard work. You must follow what the diet tells you strictly. You must do the things the book goes through, or else you would fail to achieve the weight loss that you desire to achieve. It is easy to find the instance that the conventional methods of dieting could work better for some. However, when you are committed to a diet like this, you can achieve your goals, and you can achieve them in harder ways.

So the ketogenic diet is an effective way to lose weight. It is a very good way if you want to lose excess weight. But it can be time-consuming. It can be restrictive and difficult to maintain, especially for those individuals who are naturally thin and have never dieted in their lives. But ketosis is the underlying reason why it works so well. If you want to lose weight by ketosis, this diet is right for you. But you will have to stick with it for a while. If you stick with it, you will get the result.

1. THE KETOGENIC DIET

The health benefits of the Keto diet are not different for men or women, but the speed at which they are reached does differ. As mentioned, human bodies are a lot different when it comes to how they can to burn fats and lose weight. For example, by design, women have at least 10% more body fat than men. No matter how fit you are, this is just an aspect of being a human that you must consider. Don't be hard on yourself if you notice that it seems like men can lose weight easier, that's because they can! What women have in additional body fat, men typically have the same in muscle mass. This is why men tend to see faster external results because that added muscle mass means that their metabolism rates are higher. That increased metabolism means that fat and energy get burned faster. When you are on Keto, though, the internal change is happening right away.

Your metabolism is unique, but it is also going to be slower than a man's by nature. Since muscle is able to burn more calories than fat, the weight just seems to fall off of men, giving them the ability to reach the opportunity for muscle growth quickly. This should not be something that holds you back from starting your Keto journey. As long as you keep these realistic bodily factors in mind, you won't be left wondering why it is taking you a little bit longer to start losing weight. This point will come for you, but it will take a little bit more of a process that you must be committed to following through with.

Another unique condition that a woman can experience but a man cannot is PCOS or Polycystic Ovary Syndrome; a hormonal imbalance that causes the development of cysts. These cysts can cause pain, interfere with normal reproductive function, burst extreme and dangerous cases. PCOS is actually very common among women, affecting up to 10% of the entire female population. Surprisingly, most women are not even aware that they have the condition. Around 70% of women have PCOS, which is undiagnosed. This condition can cause a significant hormonal imbalance, therefore affecting your metabolism. It can also inevitably lead to weight gain, making it even harder to see results while following diet plans. In order to stay on top of your health, you must make sure that you are going to the gynecologist regularly.

Menopause is another reality that must be faced by women, especially as we age. Most women begin the process of menopause in their mid-40s. Men do not go through menopause, so they are spared from another condition that causes slower metabolism and weight gain. When you start menopause, it is easy to gain weight and lose muscle. Most women, once menopause begins, lose muscle at a much faster rate and conversely gain weight, despite dieting and exercise regimens. Keto can, therefore, be the right diet plan for you. Regardless of what your body is doing naturally, via processes like menopause, your internal systems are still going to be making the switch from running on carbs to deriving energy from fats.

When the body begins to run on fats successfully, you have an automatic fuel reserving waiting to be burned. It will take some time for your body to do this, but when it does, you can eat fewer calories and still feel just as full because your body knows to take energy from the fat you already have. This will become automatic. However, it is a process that requires some patience, but being aware of what is actually going on with your body can help you stay motivated while on Keto.

Because a Keto diet reduces the amount of sugar you are consuming, it naturally lowers the amount of insulin in your bloodstream. This can actually have amazing effects on any existing PCOS and fertility issues, as well as menopausal symptoms and conditions like pre-diabetes and Type 2 diabetes. Once your body adjusts to a Keto diet, you are overcoming things that are naturally in place that prevent you from losing weight and getting healthy. Even if you placed your body on a strict diet, if it isn't getting rid of sugars properly, you likely aren't going to see the same results that you will when you try Keto. This is a big reason why Keto can be so beneficial for women.

You might not even realize that your hormones are not in the balance until you experience a lifestyle that limits carbs and eliminates sugars. Keto is going to reset this balance for you, keeping your hormones at healthy levels. As a result of this, you will probably find yourself in a better general mood and with much more energy to get through your days.

For people over 50, there are guidelines to follow when you start your Keto diet. As long as you follow the method properly and listen to what your body truly needs, you should have no more problems than men do while following the plan. What you will have are more obstacles to overcome, but you can do it. Remember that plenty of women successfully follow a Keto diet and see great results. Use these women as inspiration for how you anticipate your own journey to go. On the days when it seems impossible, remember what you have working against you, but more importantly, what you have working for you. Your body is designed to go into ketogenesis more than it is designed to store fat by overeating carbs. Use this as a motivation to keep pushing you ahead. Keto is a valid option for you, and the results will prove this, especially if you are over the age of 50.

2. CHALLENGES SENIORS OVER 50 FACES DURING THE KETO DIET AND HOW TO AVOID THEM

The keto diet for women after 50 is a challenge for many seniors. The goal of the keto diet is to lower carbohydrate intake and replace those calories with healthy fats. To comply with this low-carb, high-fat (LCHF) diet, you need to cut back on pasta and bread – which are common staples in the American diet. But don't fret! There are plenty of modifications that can be made to a keto food plan to suit your needs as an older woman.

Here are some of the challenges that women over 50 years may face while on keto diet:

1. Low Energy

The keto diet is great for weight loss, but for some older women, it might lower energy and some feel weak during the day. A good solution to this problem is to lower your carb intake to 50 grams per day. This will improve your energy levels and reduce any hunger cravings you have during the day.

2. High Blood Pressure

The keto diet can increase blood pressure in some cases because of its high-fat content. To prevent an increase in blood pressure, try adding more low-carb vegetables into your daily meals and avoid salt while seasoning your foods with herbs or spices instead. Adding too much salt can also increase the risk of heart disease on a keto diet plan.

3. Constipation

Reduced carbohydrate intake can contribute to constipation, and keep in mind that a lower fiber diet also makes it more likely you'll become dehydrated. If you have this problem, try adding more fiber-rich foods to your keto diet plan – such as avocado, low-sugar fruits, nuts, or seeds. A high-fiber diet will help to ensure that waste is eliminated naturally from your body.

4. Weak Bones

Many older women are at risk for osteoporosis because of the slower metabolism that occurs with age. To avoid becoming weak and fragile, be sure to get enough calcium while following a keto diet plan for women over 50 years of age. Dairy products such as cheese and yogurt are the best source of calcium. You should not take calcium supplements, however, if you have kidney issues or are taking medication for osteoporosis or high blood pressure.

5. Constantly Hungry

While keto diet plans for seniors are effective in helping to lose weight, they might not be satiating in all cases. If you feel like you're constantly hungry – especially at night – try eating more low-carb vegetables and protein to curb your hunger. Be sure to add enough healthy fats such as butter, olive oil, and coconut oil to your meal plan as well to assure that your satiety hormones stay active and that you don't feel hungry throughout the day.

6. Bad Breath

Unfortunately, for some women, the keto diet plan can cause bad breath. One of the reasons why this happens is because a keto diet plan is very low in carbohydrates, and since bacteria feed off of carbohydrate sources, it causes less bacteria to grow in your mouth. To avoid this problem, try eating more high-fiber foods like vegetables and nuts to help feed good bacteria that keep your breath smelling fresh all day long.

7. Dry Skin

Many seniors experience dry skin due to a decline in hormones as well as slower circulation and some people on a keto diet plan often complain about dry skin as well. Dry skin can cause itchy sensations and a lack of hydration, but the good news is that you can avoid this problem by eating more healthy fats like olive oil, coconut oil, and avocado while on a keto diet plan.

8. Constipation

One of the most common side effects that people experience while on a ketogenic diet plan is constipation. This happens because keto diets contain less fiber than normal diets. The best way to avoid this problem is to add more high fiber foods such as nuts & seeds, low sugar fruits, and leafy vegetables into your daily meals. Also be sure to drink plenty of water throughout the day to stay hydrated and regular.

9. Hair Loss

Another common side effect of ketogenic diet plans is hair loss. Like constipation, hair loss is also caused by a lack of fiber in your diet. You can prevent this problem by providing your body with plenty of nutrition, as well as by consuming enough water and adding fiber rich foods into your daily meals such as nuts, seeds, leafy green vegetables, and avocados.

10. Dry Mouth and Mouth Ulcers

A keto diet plan can cause dry mouth and mouth ulcers, this is because when the keto diet causes a decrease in carbohydrate intake, it also reduces the body's production of saliva (the watery part of the bodily fluid). Saliva helps to eliminate bacteria from your mouth. To reduce symptoms of dry mouth and mouth ulcers, make sure you drink plenty of fluids throughout the day and add more high-fiber foods like vegetables into your diet.

If you are over 50 years old and are thinking about trying a ketogenic diet plan, remember to consult with your physician first for any medical conditions you might have before starting this low-carb meal plan. The following list gives you the 10 most common side effects that occur with a keto diet. However, some of the symptoms might not necessarily happen to you or might occur at a different intensity. If you are experiencing any of these side effects, remember to consult with your doctor before starting a keto diet plan for seniors or women over 50 years of age to make sure you're getting all of the nutrition your body needs.

3. FOODS ALLOWED IN THE KETO DIET

Keto is best known for being a low-carb diet. But what kind of foods can you eat on the keto diet? And what are you supposed to stay away from? To answer these questions, we have put together this guide to all the keto-approved foods!

Keep in mind that there are certain foods that fall into grey areas of the keto diet. Foods such as dairy products, legumes, and potatoes all fall into this category. These foods are still low-carb, but you should use them in moderation. Read on to find out what you can eat and what you should avoid on the keto diet!

What to Eat on the Keto Diet?

The keto diet is a very low-carb diet. Carbs are kept very low in order to force your body to burn fat for fuel instead of carbohydrates (sugar). This process results in ketosis: when there is not enough glucose (sugar) for energy, your body burns its own fats for energy instead. There are two types of ketones: acetoacetate and beta-hydroxybutyrate, which are produced by your liver. The former is bad for your body and can cause ketoacidosis, while the latter is beneficial and produces energy. This is why it's important to keep an eye on your glucose levels when entering a state of ketosis.

When in ketosis, your body changes its fuel supply to run almost entirely on fat. This reduces insulin levels (which lowers fat storage) and means you are burning more calories than you are consuming; both very good things for weight loss!

To enter a state of ketosis, start by cutting out all sugars from your diet. If you are a sugar-holic, this can definitely be hard to do. But by limiting your carb intake, and therefore your energy supply, you will soon find yourself feeling more energised by just eating clean whole foods.

Keto Diet Foods: What to Eat

A keto diet has been proven to work for weight loss and improving your general health. For this reason, many people choose to follow the diet on a regular basis. We have already looked at the most important factor of keto: limiting carbs! Now we have a look at all the most important foods to consume in order to be successful on the keto diet.

Meat

Protein is an essential part of the keto diet. Eating protein helps to keep you full and increases your metabolic rate. Keto-approved meats include chicken, beef, lamb, turkey, duck and others. Eggs are also great for keto diets – they have a high protein content and use the fat within them for cooking. You can purchase organic meat at the grocery store or farmer's market instead of eating factory farmed meat that has been treated with antibiotics and hormones.

Fish/Seafood

Fish are good sources of protein. They are also rich in omega-3 fatty acids, which are naturally found in the diet. Oily fish such as salmon, mackerel and herring are great choices. Seafood high in omega-3's include crab, shrimp and krill.

Vegetables

Vegetables are important on the keto diet on account of their Fibre content. Eating lots of fibrous vegetables will help you to feel fuller for longer and promotes good gut health. Keto-friendly vegetables include spinach, broccoli, green beans, lettuce and asparagus.

Low-Carb Fruits

Fruits are a little more controversial when it comes to the keto diet. On one hand, they are extremely healthy thanks to their antioxidant content. On the other hand, they contain a lot of sugar and carbohydrates. As long as you keep your fruit intake under control, you should be fine on the keto diet. We recommend that you eat berries in moderation and avoid fruits with seeds such as bananas or oranges.

Dairy Products

Some people find that dairy products help them to be successful within their keto diet. However, low-fat or fat-free options are best because they offer fewer carbohydrates while still remaining high in protein and vitamins. Whole milk is not a good idea when on keto because it is high in fat and has lots of carbs.

Nuts and Seeds

Keto-friendly nuts and seeds include macadamia nuts, walnuts, pecans, almonds and flaxseeds. These are high in fats and protein, but low in carbohydrates.

Condiments/Spices/Other Additions to Food

There are all kinds of sauces that you can add to your meat to make it taste better. Additionally, you can add different spices to your meat before cooking it as well. For the best flavor, you should brush olive oil on the outside of your meat before cooking. This will make the meat more tasteful and also allow it to cook better.

Other keto-friendly condiments include mustard, mayonnaise, barbecue sauce, garlic salt and pepper. Bacon is a great addition to any meal once on the keto diet. Use full-fat cheese sparingly or only when in moderation because it's high in fat and carbs. Use salt and pepper sparingly as well – they're high in sodium which can create excess fluid retention.

4. WHAT DOES THE KETOGENIC DIET MEAN TO WOMEN AFTER 50?

Why Keto for Women?

As we've deliberated, carbs and sugar can have a huge impact on your hormonal balance. You might not even realize that your hormones are not in balance until you experience a lifestyle that limits carbs and eliminates sugars. Keto is going to reset this balance for you, keeping your hormones at healthy levels. As a result of this, you will probably find yourself in a better general mood, and with much more energy to get through your days.

Why Keto for the Over-50s?

Why Keto for the over-50s?

As we age, we naturally look for ways to hold onto our youth and energy. It's not uncommon to think about things that promote anti-aging. Products and lifestyle changes are advertised everywhere, and they are designed to catch your attention, as you grapple with the reality of what it means to be a 50++-year-old woman in our society. Even if you aren't eating for anti-aging purposes yet, you have likely thought about it in terms of the way you treat your skin and hair, for example. The great thing about the Keto diet is that it supports maximum health, from the inside out; working hard to make sure that you are in the best shape that you can be in.

For instance, indigestion becomes as common as you age. This happens because the body is not able to break down certain foods as well as it used to. With all of the additives and fillers, we all become used to putting our bodies through discomfort in an attempt to digest regular meals. You are probably not even aware that you are doing this to your body, but upon trying a Keto diet, you will realize how your digestion will begin to change. You will no longer feel bloated or uncomfortable after you eat. If you notice this as a common feeling, you are likely not eating food that is nutritious enough to satisfy your needs and is only resulting in excess calories.

Keto fills you up in all of the ways that you need, allowing your body to digest and metabolize all of the nutrients. When you eat your meals, you should not feel the need to overeat in order to overcompensate for not having enough nutrients. Anything that takes stress off of any system in your body is going to become a form of anti-aging. You will quickly find this benefit once you start your Keto journey, as it is one of the first-reported changes that most participants notice. In addition to a healthier digestive system, you will also experience more regular bathroom usage, with little to none of the problems often associated with age.

While weight loss is one of the more common desires for most 50+ women who start a diet plan, the way that the weight is lost matters. If you have ever shed a lot of weight before, you have probably experienced the adverse effects of sagging or drooping skin that you were left to deal with. Keto actually rejuvenates the elasticity in your skin. This means that you will be able to lose weight, and your skin will be able to catch up. Instead of having to do copious amounts of exercise to firm up your skin, it should already be becoming firmer each day you are on the Keto diet. This is something that a lot of participants are pleasantly surprised to find out.

Women also commonly report a natural reduction in wrinkles and healthier skin and hair growth, in general. Many women who start the diet report that they actually notice reverse effects in their aging process. While the skin becomes healthier and suppler, it also becomes firmer. Even if you aren't presently losing weight, you will still be able to appreciate the effects that Keto brings to your skin and face. Because your internal systems are becoming healthier by the day, this tends to show on the outside in a short amount of time. You will also begin to feel healthier. While it is possible to read about the experiences of others, there is nothing like feeling this for yourself when you begin Keto.

Everyone, especially women over 50, has day-to-day tasks draining and require certain amounts of energy to complete. Aging can, unfortunately, take away from your energy reserve, even if you get enough sleep at night. It limits the way you have to live your life, and this can become a very frustrating realization. Most diet plans bring about a sluggish feeling that you are simply supposed to get used to, for example. But Keto does the exact opposite. When you change your eating habits to fit the Keto guidelines, you are going to be hit with a boost of energy. Since your body is truly getting everything that it needs nutritionally, it will repay you with a sustained energy supply.

Another common complaint about women over 50 is that seemingly overnight, your blood sugar levels are going to be more sensitive than usual. While it is important that everyone keeps an eye on these levels, it is especially important for those in their 50s and beyond. High blood sugar can be an indication that diabetes is on the way, but Keto can become a preventative measure, that we've already talked about. Additionally, naturally regulating elevated blood sugar levels, also reduces systemic inflammation, which is also common for women over 50. By balancing the immune system, of which inflammation is a part of, common aches and pains are reduced. Inflammation can also affect vital organs and is a precursor to cancer. Keto will support your path to an anti-inflammatory lifestyle.

Sugar is never great for us, but it turns out that sugar can become especially dangerous as we age. What is known as a "sugar sag" can occur when you get older because the excess sugar molecules will attach themselves to skin and protein in your body. This doesn't even necessarily happen because you are eating too much sugar. Average levels of sugar intake can also lead to this sagging as the sugar weakens the strength of your proteins that are supposed to hold you together. With sagging comes even more wrinkles and arterial stiffening.

If you have any anti-aging concerns, the Keto diet will likely be able to address your worries. It is a diet that works extremely hard while allowing you a fairly simple and direct guideline to follow in return. While your motivation is necessary in order to form a successful relationship with Keto, you won't need to worry about doing anything "wrong" or accidentally breaking from your diet. As long as you know how to give up your sugary foods and drinks while making sure that you are consuming the correct amount of carbs, you will be able to find your own success while on a diet.

As a woman over 50, you'll find that you will feel better, healthier and younger, by implementing the simple steps that will tune your body into processing excess fats for energy. You'll build muscle, lose fat, and look and feel younger. As we've touched on, a Keto diet helps balance your hormones, reversing and/or eliminating many common menopausal signs and symptoms.

5. HOW THE KETOGENIC DIET HELPS WITH THE SIGN AND SYMPTOMS OF AGEING AND MENOPAUSE

For ageing women, menopause will bring severe changes and challenges, but the ketogenic diet can help you switch gears effortlessly to continue enjoying a healthy and happy life. Menopause can upset hormonal levels in women, which consequently affects brainpower and cognitive abilities. Furthermore, due to less production of estrogens and progesterone, your sex drive declines, and you suffer from sleep issues and mood problems. Let's have a look at how a ketogenic diet will help solve these side effects.

- Enhanced cognitive functions: Usually, hormone estrogen ensures continuous flow of glucose into your brain. But after menopause, the estrogen levels begin to drop dramatically, so does the amount of glucose reaching the bran. As a result, your functional brainpower will start to deteriorate. However, by following the keto diet for women over 50, the problem of glucose intake is circumvented. This results in enhanced cognitive functions and brain activity.

- Hormonal balance: Usually, women face major symptoms of menopause due to hormonal imbalances. The keto diet for women over 50 works by stabilizing these imbalances such as estrogen; this aids in experiencing fewer and bearable menopausal symptoms like hot flashes. The keto diet also balances blood sugar levels and insulin and helps in controlling insulin sensitivity.

- Intensified sex drive: The keto diet surges the absorption of vitamin D, which is essential for enhancing sex drive. Vitamin D ensures stable levels of testosterone and other sex hormones that could become unstable due to low levels of testosterone.

- Better sleep: Glucose disturbs your blood sugar levels dramatically, which in turn leads to poor quality of sleep. Along with other menopausal symptoms, good sleep becomes a huge problem as you age. The keto diet for women over 50 not only balances blood glucose levels, but also stabilizes other hormones like cortisol, melatonin, and serotonin warranting an improved and better sleep.

- Reduces inflammation: Menopause can upsurge the inflammation levels by letting potential harmful invaders in our system, which result in uncomfortable and painful symptoms. Keto diet for women over 50 uses the healthy anti-inflammatory fats to reduce inflammation and lower pain in your joints and bones.

- Fuel your brain: Are you aware that your brain is composed of 60% fat or more? This infers that it needs a larger amount of fat to keep it functioning optimally. In other words, the ketones from the keto diet serve as the energy source that fuels your brain cells.

- Nutrient deficiencies: Ageing women tend to have higher deficiencies in essential nutrients such as, iron deficiency which leads to brain fog and fatigue; vitamin B12 deficiency, which leads to neurological conditions like dementia; fats deficiency, that can lead to problems with cognition, skin, vision; and vitamin D deficiency that not only causes cognitive impairment in older adults and increase the risk of heart disease but also contribute to the risk of developing cancer. On a keto diet, the high-quality proteins ensure adequate and excellent sources of these important nutrients.

- Controlling Blood Sugar: Research has suggested a link between poor blood sugar levels and brain diseases such as Alzheimer's disease, Parkinson's disease, or Dementia. Some factors contributing to Alzheimer's disease may include:

- Enormous intake of carbohydrates, especially from fructose—which is drastically reduced in the ketogenic diet.

- Lack of nutritional fats and good cholesterol—which are copious and healthy in the keto diet

The Keto Diet helps control blood sugar and improve nutrition; which in turn not only improves insulin response and resistance, but also protects against memory loss which is often a part of ageing.

6. BREAKFAST RECIPES

PREPARATION: 5 MIN

COOKING: 15 MIN

SERVES: 1

1. KETO-FLU COMBAT SMOOTHIE

INGREDIENTS

- ½ cup unsweetened nut or seed milk (hemp, almond, coconut, and cashew)
- 1 cup spinach
- ½ medium avocado (about 75 grams), pitted and peeled
- 1 scoop MCT powder (or 1 tablespoon MCT oil)
- ½ tablespoon unsweetened cacao powder
- ¼ teaspoon of sea salt
- Dash sweetener (optional)
- ½ cup ice

DIRECTIONS

1. In a blender, combine the milk, spinach, avocado, MCT powder, cacao powder, salt, sweetener (if using), and ice and blend until smooth.

NUTRITION

- Calories: 249
- Total fat: 21g
- Protein: 5g
- Total carbs: 10g
- Fiber: 8g
- Net carbs: 2g

PREPARATION: 5 MIN

COOKING: 15 MIN

SERVES: 1

2. STRAWBERRIES AND CREAM SMOOTHIE

INGREDIENTS

- 5 medium strawberries, hulled
- 3 tablespoons heavy (whipping) cream
- 3 ice cubes
- Your favorite vanilla-flavored sweetener

DIRECTIONS

1. In a blender, combine all the ingredients and blend until smooth. Enjoy right away!

NUTRITION

- Calories: 176
- Total fat: 16g
- Protein: 2g
- Total carbs: 6g
- Fiber: 1g
- Net carbs: 5g

PREPARATION: 10 MINUTES PLUS OVERNIGHT TO CHILL.

COOKING: 20 MIN

SERVES: 12 BARS

3. NO-BAKE KETO POWER BARS

INGREDIENTS

- ½ cup pili nuts
- ½ cup whole hazelnuts
- ½ cup walnut halves
- ¼ cup hulled sunflower seeds
- ¼ cup unsweetened coconut flakes or chips
- ¼ cup hulled hemp seeds
- 2 tablespoons unsweetened cacao nibs
- 2 scoops collagen powder (I use 1 scoop Perfect Keto vanilla collagen and 1 scoop Perfect Keto unflavored collagen powder)
- ½ teaspoon ground cinnamon
- ½ teaspoon sea salt
- ¼ cup coconut oil, melted
- 1 teaspoon vanilla extract
- Stevia or monk fruit to sweeten (optional if you are using unflavored collagen powder)

DIRECTIONS

1. Line a 9-inch square baking pan with parchment paper.
2. In a food processor or blender, combine the pili nuts, hazelnuts, walnuts, sunflower seeds, coconut, hemp seeds, cacao nibs, collagen powder, cinnamon, and salt and pulse a few times.
3. Add the coconut oil, vanilla extract, and sweetener (if using). Pulse again until the ingredients are combined. Do not over pulse, or it will turn to mush. You want the nuts and seeds to have some texture.
4. Pour the mixture into the prepared pan and press it into an even layer. Cover with another piece of parchment (or fold over extra from the first piece) and place a heavy pan or dish on top to help press the bars together.
5. Refrigerate overnight and then cut into 12 bars. Store the bars in individual storage bags in the refrigerator for a quick grab-and-go breakfast.

NUTRITION

- Calories: 242
- Total fat: 22g
- Protein: 6.5g
- Total carbs: 4.5g
- Fiber: 2.5g
- Net carbs: 2g

PREPARATION: 10 MIN

COOKING: 20 MIN

SERVES: 4

4. BACON CHEESEBURGER WAFFLES

INGREDIENTS

- Pepper and salt to taste
- 3 ounces of cheddar cheese
- 4 tablespoons of sugar-free barbecue sauce
- 4 slices of bacon
- 4 ounces of ground beef, 70% lean meat and 30% fat
- Waffle dough:
- Pepper and salt to taste
- 3 tablespoons parmesan cheese, grated
- 4 tablespoons almond flour
- ¼ teaspoon onion powder
- ¼ teaspoon garlic powder
- 1 cup (125 grams) of cauliflower crumbles
- 2 large eggs
- Ounces of cheddar cheese

DIRECTIONS

1. Shred about 3 ounces of cheddar cheese, then add in cauliflower crumbles in a bowl and put in half of the cheddar cheese.
2. Put into the mixture spices, almond flour, eggs and parmesan cheese, then mix and put aside for some time.
3. Thinly slice the bacon and cook in a skillet on medium to high heat.
4. After the bacon is cooked partially, put in the beef; cook until the mixture is well done.
5. Then put the excess grease from the bacon mixture into the waffle mixture. Set aside the bacon mix.
6. Use an immersion blender to blend the waffle mix until it becomes a paste, then add the waffle iron half of the mix and cook until it becomes crispy.
7. Repeat for the remaining waffle mixture.
8. As the waffles cook, add sugar-free barbecue sauce to the ground beef and bacon mixture in the skillet.
9. Then proceed to assemble waffles by topping them with half of the left cheddar cheese and half the beef mixture. Repeat this for the remaining waffles, broil for around 1–2 minutes until the cheese has melted, then serve right away.

NUTRITION

- Protein: 18.8g
- Fats: 33.94g
- Calories: 405.25
- Carbs: 4.35g

PREPARATION: 20 MIN

COOKING: 45 MIN

SERVES: 24 MINI CHEESECAKE

5. KETO BREAKFAST CHEESECAKE

INGREDIENTS

Toppings:
- 1/4 cup mixed berries for each cheesecake, frozen and thawed

Filling ingredients:
- 1/2 teaspoon vanilla extract
- 1/2 teaspoon almond extract
- 3/4 cup sweetener
- 6 eggs
- 8 ounces cream cheese
- 16 ounces cottage cheese

Crust ingredients:
- 4 tablespoons salted butter
- 2 tablespoons sweetener
- 2 cups almonds, whole

DIRECTIONS

1. Preheat oven to 350°F.
2. Pulse almonds in a food processor, then add in butter and sweetener.
3. Pulse until all the ingredients mix well and a course dough is formed.
4. Coat twelve silicone muffin pans using foil or paper liners.
5. Divide the batter between the muffin pans, then press into the bottom part until it forms a crust and bake for about 8 minutes.
6. In the meantime, mix in a food processor the cream cheese and cottage cheese, then pulse until the mixture is smooth.
7. Put in the extracts and sweetener, then combine until well mixed.
8. Add in eggs and pulse again until it becomes smooth; you might need to scrape down the mixture from the sides of the processor. Share the batter between the muffin pans and then bake for around 30–40 minutes until the middle is not wobbly when you shake the muffin pan lightly.
9. Put aside until cooled completely, then put in the refrigerator for about 2 hours and then top with frozen and thawed berries.

NUTRITION

- Fats: 12g
- Calories: 152
- Proteins: 6g
- Carbs: 3g

PREPARATION: 5 MIN

COOKING: 15 MIN

SERVES: 5 ROLL-UPS

6. BREAKFAST ROLL-UPS

INGREDIENTS

- Nonstick cooking spray
- 5 patties of cooked breakfast sausage
- 5 slices of cooked bacon
- 2 Cups of cheddar cheese, shredded
- Pepper and salt
- 10 large eggs

DIRECTIONS

1. Preheat a skillet on medium to high heat, then use a whisk and combine together two of the eggs in a mixing bowl.
2. After the pan has become hot, lower the heat to medium-low heat, then put in the eggs. If you want to, you can utilize some cooking spray.
3. Season the eggs with some pepper and salt.
4. Cover the eggs and leave them to cook for a couple of minutes or until the eggs are almost cooked.
5. Drizzle around 1/3 cup of cheese on top of the eggs, then place a strip of bacon and divide the sausage into two and place on top.
6. Roll the egg carefully on top of the fillings. The roll-up will almost look like a taquito. If you have a hard time folding over the egg, use a spatula to keep the egg intact until the egg has been molded into a roll-up.
7. Put aside the roll-up, then repeat the above steps until you have four more roll-ups; you should have 5 roll-ups in total.

NUTRITION

- Calories: 412.2
- Fats: 31.66g
- Carbs: 2.26g
- Proteins: 28.21g

PREPARATION: 20 MIN

COOKING: 35 MIN

SERVES: 12 ROLLS

7. BASIC OPIE ROLLS

INGREDIENTS

- 1/8 teaspoon salt
- 1/8 teaspoon cream of tartar
- 3 ounces cream cheese
- 3 large eggs

DIRECTIONS

1. Preheat the oven to about 300°F, then separate the egg whites from the egg yolks and place both eggs in different bowls. Using an electric mixer, beat well the egg whites, until the mixture is very bubbly, then add in the cream of tartar and mix again until it forms a stiff peak.
2. In the bowl with the egg yolks, put in 3 ounces of cubed cheese and salt. Mix well until the mixture has doubled in size and is pale yellow. Put in the egg white mixture into the egg yolk mixture, then fold the mixture together.
3. Spray some oil on the cookie sheet coated with some parchment paper, then add dollops of the batter and bake for around 30 minutes.
4. You will know they are ready when the upper part of the rolls is firm and golden. Leave them to cool for a few minutes on a wire rack. Enjoy with some coffee.

NUTRITION

- Calories: 45
- Fats: 4g
- Proteins: 2g

PREPARATION: 5 MIN

COOKING: 7 MIN

SERVES: 1

8. CREAM CHEESE PANCAKE

INGREDIENTS

- 1/2 to 1 packet of Stevia
- 1 tablespoon coconut flour
- ½ teaspoon cinnamon
- 2 eggs
- 2 ounces of cream cheese

DIRECTIONS

1. Combine well all of the ingredients in a bowl until the mixture is smooth, then heat a skillet over medium to high heat and add in coconut oil.
2. Add a scoop of the batter in the heated pan and cook for about 2 minutes on both sides. Repeat the same for the remaining batter. Top the pancakes with sugar-free maple syrup.

NUTRITION

- Calories: 365
- Fats: 19g
- Carbs: 8g
- Proteins: 17g

PREPARATION: 5 MIN

COOKING: 5 MIN

SERVES: 2

9. BLUEBERRY COCONUT PORRIDGE

INGREDIENTS

Toppings:
- 1 ounce of coconut, shaved
- 2 tablespoons pumpkin seeds
- 60 grams blueberries
- 2 tablespoons butter

Porridge:
- 1 pinch of salt
- 10 drops of liquid stevia
- 1 teaspoon vanilla extract
- 1 teaspoon cinnamon
- 1/4 cup coconut flour
- 1/4 cup flaxseed, ground
- 1 cup almond milk

DIRECTIONS

1. Let the almond milk heat up over low heat, put in salt, cinnamon, coconut flour, and flaxseed, then combine well.
2. Use a whisk to get rid of any clumps.
3. Then heat the mixture until it slightly bubbles before adding in vanilla extract and liquid stevia.
4. When the almond mixture becomes as thick as you like, switch off the heat and put in the toppings.

NUTRITION

- Calories: 405
- Fats: 34g
- Carbs: 8g
- Proteins: 10g

PREPARATION: 10 MIN

COOKING: 20 MIN

SERVES: 4

10. CAULIFLOWER HASH BROWNS

INGREDIENTS

- 4 ounces of butter to be used for frying
- 2 pinches of pepper
- 1 teaspoon of salt
- ½ grated yellow onion
- 3 eggs
- 15 ounces of cauliflower

DIRECTIONS

1. Rinse with some water, trim and grate the cauliflower with a grater or food processor.
2. Put the cauliflower in a bowl, then add in the remaining ingredients and combine before putting aside for about 5–10 minutes.
3. In a skillet, on medium heat, melt some oil or butter, then keep the oven over low heat to ensure that the first set of pancakes are still warm as you make the rest.
4. Put a scoop of the batter in the skillet and flatten it until it measures around 3–4 inches in thickness.
5. Fry for around 4–5 minutes on every side; regulate the heat to ensure that the pancakes do not burn. Repeat the same for the remaining batter.

NUTRITION

- Carbs: 5g
- Proteins: 7g
- Calories: 278g
- Fats: 26g

PREPARATION: 10 MIN

COOKING: 12 MIN

SERVES: 8-10

11. KETO ROLLS

INGREDIENTS

Filling:
- 2 teaspoons cinnamon
- 3 tablespoons melted butter

Frosting:
- 1 squeeze of liquid stevia
- 1 tablespoon lemon juice
- ¼ cup butter, room temperature
- 2 tablespoons vanilla extract
- 4 tablespoons cream cheese

Dough:
- 2 squeezes of liquid stevia
- 1 whisked egg
- ½ teaspoon cinnamon
- 3 ounces cream cheese
- 1(½) cups mozzarella
- 1(¼) cups almond flour

DIRECTIONS

1. Preheat the oven to about 400°F.
2. In a small bowl, put in cream and mozzarella cheese, then microwave the cheese mixture for around a minute; remove it and mix well.
3. Place the cheese mixture into the microwave for one more minute and mix again, then put in the egg, cinnamon, stevia and almond flour. Stir well to combine.
4. The mixture might be a little wet, but if it very wet and sticking on your fingers, then you can add some more flour. Roll out the dough using a rolling pin, then spread onto the batter the butter and drizzle some cinnamon.
5. Roll up the batter from one end to the other until you get a cylinder shape. With a pizza cutter or knife, slice the rolled dough into pieces and put these pieces on a baking sheet coated with parchment paper.
6. Bake for about 10–12 minutes at 400°F.
7. In the meantime, prepare the frosting. In a mixing bowl, put in butter and cream cheese and combine until the mixture is creamy, add in lemon juice and vanilla extract. Combine well until everything is incorporated.
8. When the rolls are ready, add the frosting on each roll; you can add the frosting on the rolls immediately or after about 5–10 minutes.

NUTRITION

- Carbs: 5g
- Calories: 320
- Protein: 11g
- Fat: 29g

PREPARATION: 10 MIN | **COOKING: 40 MIN** | **SERVES: 3**

12. NUT GRANOLA & SMOOTHIE BOWL

INGREDIENTS

- 6 cups Greek yogurt
- 4 tablespoon almond butter
- A handful toasted walnuts
- 3 tablespoon unsweetened cocoa powder
- 4 teaspoon swerve brown sugar
- 2 cups nut granola for topping

DIRECTIONS

1. Combine the Greek yogurt, almond butter, walnuts, cocoa powder, and swerve brown sugar in a smoothie maker; puree in high-speed until smooth and well mixed.
2. Share the smoothie into four breakfast bowls, top with a half cup of granola each, and serve.

NUTRITION

- Calories: 361
- Fat 31.2g
- Net carbs 2g
- Protein 13g

PREPARATION: 10 MIN

COOKING: 30 MIN

SERVES: 3

13. BACON AND EGG QUESADILLAS

INGREDIENTS

- 8 low carb tortilla shells
- 6 eggs
- 1 cup water
- 3 tablespoon butter
- 1 ½ cups grated cheddar cheese
- 1 ½ cups grated Swiss cheese
- 5 bacon slices
- 1 medium onion, thinly sliced
- 1 tablespoon chopped parsley

DIRECTIONS

1. Bring the eggs to a boil in water over medium heat for 10 minutes. Transfer the eggs to an ice water bath, peel the shells, and chop them; set aside.
2. Meanwhile, as the eggs cook, fry the bacon in a skillet over medium heat for 4 minutes until crispy. Remove and chop. Plate and set aside too.
3. Fetch out 2/3 of the bacon fat and sauté the onions in the remaining grease over medium heat for 2 minutes; set aside. Melt 1 tablespoon of butter in a skillet over medium heat.
4. Lay one tortilla in a skillet; sprinkle with some Swiss cheese. Add some chopped eggs and bacon over the cheese, top with onion, and sprinkle with some cheddar cheese. Cover with another tortilla shell. Cook for 45 seconds, then carefully flip the quesadilla, and cook the other side too for 45 seconds. Remove to a plate and repeat the cooking process using the remaining tortilla shells.
5. Garnish with parsley and serve warm.

NUTRITION

- Calories: 449
- Fat 48.7g
- Net Carbs 6.8g
- Protein 29.1g

PREPARATION: 10 MIN   **COOKING: 20 MIN**   **SERVES: 3**

14. SPICY EGG MUFFINS WITH BACON & CHEESE

INGREDIENTS

- 12 eggs
- ¼ cup coconut milk
- Salt and black pepper to taste
- 1 cup grated cheddar cheese
- 12 slices bacon
- 4 jalapeño peppers, seeded and minced

DIRECTIONS

1. Preheat the oven to 370°F.
2. Crack the eggs into a bowl and whisk with coconut milk until combined. Season with salt and pepper, and evenly stir in the cheddar cheese.
3. Line each hole of a muffin tin with a slice of bacon and fill each with the egg mixture two-thirds way up. Top with the jalapeno peppers and bake in the oven for 18 to 20 minutes or until puffed and golden. Remove, allow cooling for a few minutes, and serve with arugula salad.

NUTRITION

- Calories: 302
- Fat: 23.7g
- Net Carbs: 3.2g
- Protein: 20g

 **PREPARATION: 10 MIN**  **COOKING: 25 MIN**  **SERVES: 3**

15. DARK CHOCOLATE SMOOTHIE

INGREDIENTS

- 8 pecans
- ¾ cup coconut milk
- ¼ cup water
- 1 ½ cups watercress
- 2 teaspoon vegan protein powder
- 1 tablespoon chia seeds
- 1 tablespoon unsweetened cocoa powder
- 4 fresh dates, pitted

DIRECTIONS

1. In a blender, add all ingredients and process until creamy and uniform. Place into two glasses and chill before serving.

NUTRITION

- Calories: 335
- Fat: 31.7g
- Net Carbs: 12.7g
- Protein: 7g

PREPARATION: 10 MIN **COOKING: 25 MIN** **SERVES: 3**

16. FIVE GREENS SMOOTHIE

INGREDIENTS

- 6 kale leaves, chopped
- 3 stalks celery, chopped
- 1 ripe avocado, skinned, pitted, sliced
- 1 cup ice cubes
- 2 cups spinach, chopped
- 1 large cucumber, peeled and chopped
- Chia seeds to garnish

DIRECTIONS

1. In a blender, add the kale, celery, avocado, and ice cubes, and blend for 45 seconds. Add the spinach and cucumber, and process for another 45 seconds until smooth.
2. Pour the smoothie into glasses, garnish with chia seeds and serve the drink immediately.

NUTRITION

- Calories: 124
- Fat: 7.8g
- Net Carbs: 2.9g
- Protein: 3.2g

PREPARATION: 10 MIN **COOKING: 25 MIN** **SERVES: 3**

17. ALMOND WAFFLES WITH CINNAMON CREAM

INGREDIENTS

For the spread:
- 8 ounces cream cheese, at room temperature
- 1 teaspoon cinnamon powder
- 3 tablespoon swerve brown sugar
- Cinnamon powder for garnishing

For the waffles:
- 5 tablespoon melted butter
- 1(½) cups unsweetened almond milk
- 7 large eggs
- ¼ teaspoon liquid stevia
- ½ teaspoon baking powder
- 1(½) cups almond flour

DIRECTIONS

1. Combine the cream cheese, cinnamon, and swerve with a hand mixer until smooth. Cover and chill until ready to use.
2. To make the waffles, whisk the butter, milk, and eggs in a medium bowl. Add the stevia and baking powder and mix. Stir in the almond flour and combine until no lumps exist. Let the batter sit for 5 minutes to thicken. Spritz a waffle iron with a nonstick cooking spray.
3. Ladle a ¼ cup of the batter into the waffle iron and cook according to the manufacturer's instructions until golden, about 10 minutes in total. Repeat with the remaining batter.
4. Slice the waffles into quarters; apply the cinnamon spread in between each of two waffles and snap. Sprinkle with cinnamon powder and serve.

NUTRITION

- Calories: 307
- Fat: 24g
- Net Carbs: 8g
- Protein: 12g

 **PREPARATION: 10 MIN**

 **COOKING: 35 MIN**

 **SERVES: 4**

18. DELICIOUS POACHED EGGS

INGREDIENTS

- 6 eggs
- 1 tablespoon ghee
- 1 Serrano pepper, chopped
- 1 red bell pepper, chopped
- 3 tomatoes, chopped
- 1 white onion, chopped
- 3 garlic cloves, minced
- 1 teaspoon paprika
- 1 teaspoon cumin
- ¼ teaspoon chili powder
- 1 tablespoon cilantro, chopped
- Salt and black pepper to taste

DIRECTIONS

1. Heat up a pan with the ghee over medium heat, add onion, stir, and cook for 10 minutes.
2. Add Serrano pepper and garlic, stir, and cook for 1 minute.
3. Add red bell pepper, stir, and cook for 10 minutes.
4. Add tomatoes, salt, pepper, chili powder, cumin, and paprika, stir and cook for 10 minutes.
5. Crack eggs into the pan, season them with salt and pepper, cover pan and cook for 6 minutes more.
6. Sprinkle cilantro at the end and serve.
7. Enjoy!

NUTRITION

- Calories: 46
- Protein: 1.97 g
- Fat: 0.49 g
- Carbohydrates: 10.07 g
- Sodium: 14 mg

 **PREPARATION: 10 MIN**

 **COOKING: 20 MIN**

 SERVES: 1

19. KETO BREAKFAST BOWL

INGREDIENTS

- 4 ounces beef, ground
- 1 avocado, pitted, peeled, and chopped
- 1 yellow onion, chopped
- 8 mushrooms, sliced
- 2 eggs, whisked
- 12 black olives, pitted and sliced
- 1 tablespoon coconut oil
- ½ teaspoon smoked paprika
- Salt and black pepper to taste

DIRECTIONS

1. Heat up a pan with the coconut oil over medium heat, add onions, mushrooms, salt, and pepper, stir and cook for 5 minutes.
2. Add beef and paprika, stir, cook for 10 minutes and transfer to a bowl.
3. Heat up the pan again over medium heat, add eggs, some salt, and pepper, and scramble them.
4. Return beef mixture to pan and stir.
5. Add avocado and olives, stir and cook for 1 minute.
6. Transfer to a bowl and serve. Enjoy!

NUTRITION

- Calories: 423
- Protein: 26.07 g
- Fat: 29.87 g
- Carbohydrates: 16.04 g
- Sodium: 120 mg

 **PREPARATION: 10 MIN**
 **COOKING: 35 MIN**
 SERVES: 6

20. YUMMY EGGS AND SAUSAGES

INGREDIENTS

- 5 tablespoons ghee
- 12 eggs
- 1-ounce spinach, torn
- 12 ham slices
- 2 sausages, chopped
- 1 yellow onion, chopped
- 1 red bell pepper, chopped
- Salt and black pepper to taste

DIRECTIONS

1. Heat up a pan with 1 tablespoon ghee over medium heat, add sausages and onion, stir and cook for 5 minutes.
2. Add bell pepper, salt, and pepper, stir and cook for 3 minutes more and transfer to a bowl.
3. Melt the rest of the ghee and divide it into 12 cupcake molds.
4. Add a slice of ham in each cupcake mold, divide spinach in each and then the sausage mix.
5. Crack an egg on top, put everything in the oven and bake at 425°F for 20 minutes.
6. Leave your Keto cupcakes to cool down a bit before serving.
7. Enjoy!

NUTRITION

- Calories: 332
- Protein: 26.27 g
- Fat: 22.47 g
- Carbohydrates: 5.16 g
- Sodium: 799 mg

PREPARATION: 10 MIN

COOKING: 10 MIN

SERVES: 1

21. BREAKFAST SCRAMBLED EGGS

INGREDIENTS

- 4 bell mushrooms, chopped
- 3 eggs, whisked
- 2 ham slices, chopped
- ¼ cup red bell pepper, chopped
- ½ cup spinach, chopped
- 1 tablespoon coconut oil
- Salt and black pepper to the taste

DIRECTIONS

1. Heat up a pan with half of the oil over medium heat, add mushrooms, spinach, ham and bell pepper, stir and cook for 4 minutes.
2. Heat up another pan with the rest of the oil over medium heat, add eggs and scramble them.
3. Add veggies and ham, salt and pepper, stir, cook for 1 minute and serve.
4. Enjoy!

NUTRITION

- Calories: 594
- Protein: 38.45 g
- Fat: 44.5 g
- Carbohydrates: 11.71 g
- Sodium: 914 mg

PREPARATION: 10 MIN

COOKING: 60 MIN

SERVES: 4

22. DELICIOUS FRITTATA

INGREDIENTS

- 9 ounces spinach
- 12 eggs
- 1-ounce pepperoni
- 5 ounces mozzarella, shredded
- ½ cup parmesan, grated
- ½ cup ricotta cheese
- 1 teaspoon garlic, minced
- 4 tablespoons olive oil
- A pinch nutmeg
- Salt and black pepper to taste

DIRECTIONS

1. Squeeze liquid from spinach and put it in a bowl.
2. In another bowl, mix eggs with salt, pepper, nutmeg and garlic, and whisk well.
3. Add spinach, parmesan, and ricotta and whisk well again.
4. Pour this into a pan, sprinkle mozzarella and pepperoni on top, put in the oven, and bake at 375°F for 45 minutes.
5. Leave frittata to cool down for a few minutes before serving it.
6. Enjoy!

NUTRITION

- Calories: 704
- Protein: 49.35 g
- Fat: 50.3 g
- Carbohydrates: 12.84 g
- Sodium: 888 mg

PREPARATION: 10 MIN

COOKING: 10 MIN

SERVES: 3

23. SMOKED SALMON BREAKFAST

INGREDIENTS

- 4 eggs, whisked
- 4 ounces smoked salmon, chopped
- ½ teaspoon avocado oil
- For the sauce:
- 1 cup coconut milk
- ½ cup cashews, soaked, drained
- ¼ cup green onions, chopped
- 1 teaspoon garlic powder
- 1 tablespoon lemon juice
- Salt and black pepper to taste

DIRECTIONS

1. In your blender, mix cashews with coconut milk, garlic powder, and lemon juice and blend well.
2. Add salt, pepper, and green onions, blend again well, transfer to a bowl and keep in the fridge for now.
3. Heat up a pan with the oil over medium-low heat, add eggs, whisk a bit and cook until they are almost done.
4. Put in your preheated broiler and cook until eggs set.
5. Divide eggs on plates, top with smoked salmon, and serve with the green onion sauce on top.
6. Enjoy!

NUTRITION

- Calories: 559
- Protein: 28.03 g
- Fat: 41.69 g
- Carbohydrates: 21.03 g
- Sodium: 463 mg

PREPARATION: 10 MIN **COOKING: 25 MIN** **SERVES: 2**

24. FETA AND ASPARAGUS DELIGHT

INGREDIENTS

- 12 asparagus spears
- 1 tablespoon olive oil
- 2 green onions, chopped
- 1 garlic clove, minced
- 6 eggs
- Salt and black pepper to taste
- ½ cup feta cheese

DIRECTIONS

1. Heat up a pan with some water over medium heat, add asparagus, cook for 8 minutes, drain well, chop 2 spears, and reserve the rest.
2. Heat up a pan with the oil over medium heat, add garlic, chopped asparagus, and onions, stir, and cook for 5 minutes.
3. Add eggs, salt and pepper, stir, cover, and cook for 5 minutes.
4. Arrange the whole asparagus on top of your frittata, sprinkle cheese, put in the oven at 350°F and bake for 9 minutes.
5. Divide between plates and serve.
6. Enjoy!

NUTRITION

- Calories: 582
- Protein: 33.93 g
- Fat: 44.06 g
- Carbohydrates: 12.09 g
- Sodium: 664 mg

 **PREPARATION: 10 MIN**

 **COOKING: 4 MIN**

 **SERVES: 12**

25. SPECIAL BREAKFAST EGGS

INGREDIENTS

- 4 tea bags
- 4 tablespoons salt
- 12 eggs
- 2 tablespoons cinnamon
- 6-star anise
- 1 teaspoon black pepper
- 1 tablespoon peppercorns
- 8 cups water
- 1 cup tamari sauce

DIRECTIONS

1. Put water in a pot, add eggs, bring them to a boil over medium heat and cook until they are hard boiled.
2. Cool them down and crack them without peeling.
3. In a large pot, mix water with tea bags, salt, pepper, peppercorns, cinnamon, star anise and tamari sauce.
4. Add cracked eggs, cover pot, bring to a simmer over low heat, and cook for 30 minutes.
5. Discard tea bags.
6. Leave eggs to cool down, peel, and serve them for breakfast.
7. Enjoy!

NUTRITION

- Calories: 146
- Protein: 9.39 g
- Fat: 10.39 g
- Carbohydrates: 3.71 g
- Sodium: 2596 mg

 **PREPARATION: 10 MIN**  **COOKING: 20 MIN**  **SERVES: 4**

26. EGGS BAKED IN AVOCADOS

INGREDIENTS

- 2 avocados, cut in halves and pitted
- 4 eggs
- Salt and black pepper to the taste
- 1 tablespoon chives, chopped

DIRECTIONS

1. Scoop some flesh from the avocado halves and arrange them in a baking dish.
2. Crack an egg in each avocado, season with salt and pepper, put them in the oven at 425°F, and bake for 20 minutes.
3. Sprinkle chives at the end and serve for breakfast!
4. Enjoy!

NUTRITION

- Calories: 295
- Protein: 11.23 g
- Fat: 24.4 g
- Carbohydrates: 10.68 g
- Sodium: 110 mg

PREPARATION: 10 MIN **COOKING: 15 MIN** **SERVES: 4**

27. SHRIMP AND BACON BREAKFAST

INGREDIENTS

- 1 cup mushrooms, sliced
- 4 bacon slices, chopped
- 4 ounces smoked salmon, chopped
- 4 ounces shrimp, deveined
- Salt and black pepper to the taste
- ½ cup coconut cream

DIRECTIONS

1. Heat up a pan over medium heat, add bacon, stir and cook for 5 minutes.
2. Add mushrooms, stir and cook for 5 minutes more.
3. Add salmon, stir and cook for 3 minutes.
4. Add shrimp and cook for 2 minutes.
5. Add salt, pepper, and coconut cream, stir, cook for 1 minute, take off heat, and divide between plates.
6. Enjoy!

NUTRITION

- Calories: 277
- Protein: 16.17 g
- Fat: 22.82 g
- Carbohydrates: 3.32 g
- Sodium: 281 mg

7. LUNCH RECIPES

PREPARATION: 10 MIN **COOKING: 47 MIN** **SERVES: 3**

28. HOT BUFFALO WINGS

INGREDIENTS

- ¼ cup hot sauce
- 4 tablespoons coconut oil, plus more for rubbing on the wings
- 12 chicken wings, fresh or frozen
- 1 clove of garlic, minced
- ¼ teaspoon salt
- ¼ teaspoon paprika
- ¼ teaspoon cayenne pepper
- 1 dash of ground black pepper

DIRECTIONS

1. Preheat your oven to 400°F (200°C).
2. Evenly spread chicken wings on a wire rack placed on a baking dish (it will save wings from becoming soggy on the bottom).
3. Rub each chicken wing with olive oil and season with salt and pepper, then bake for 45 minutes, or until crispy.
4. Meanwhile, in a saucepan combine coconut oil and garlic and cook over medium heat for 1 minute, or until fragrant.
5. Remove from heat and stir in hot sauce, salt, paprika, cayenne pepper and black pepper.
6. Remove wings from the oven and transfer to a large bowl.
7. Pour hot sauce mixture over wings and toss until each wing is coated with the sauce.
8. Serve immediately.

NUTRITION

- Calories: 391
- Carbohydrates: 1g
- Fats: 33g
- Protein: 31g

PREPARATION: 10 MIN

COOKING: 0 MIN

SERVES: 3

29. TROUT AND CHILI NUTS

INGREDIENTS

- 1.5 kilograms of rainbow trout
- 300 grams shelled walnuts
- 1 bunch of parsley
- 9 cloves of garlic
- 7 tablespoons olive oil
- 2 fresh hot peppers
- Juice of 2 lemons

DIRECTIONS

1. Clean and dry the trout, then place them in a baking tray.
2. Chop the walnuts, parsley and chili peppers, then mash the garlic cloves.
3. Mix the ingredients by adding olive oil, lemon juice and a pinch of salt.
4. Stuff the trout with some of the sauce and use the rest to cover the fish.
5. Bake at 180°F for 30/40 minutes.
6. Serve the trout hot or cold.

NUTRITION

- Calories: 226
- Fat: 5g
- Fiber: 2g
- Carbs: 7g
- Protein: 8g

PREPARATION: 10 MIN

COOKING: 30 MIN

SERVES: 3

30. AVOCADO AND KALE EGGS

INGREDIENTS

- 1 teaspoon ghee
- 1 red onion, sliced
- 4 ounces chorizo, sliced into thin rounds
- 1 cup chopped kale
- 1 ripe avocado, pitted, peeled, chopped
- 4 eggs
- Salt and black pepper to season

DIRECTIONS

1. Preheat the oven to 370°F.
2. Melt ghee in a cast iron pan over medium heat and sauté the onion for 2 minutes. Add the chorizo and cook for 2 minutes more, flipping once.
3. Introduce the kale in batches with a splash of water to wilt, season lightly with salt, stir and cook for 3 minutes. Mix in the avocado and turn the heat off.
4. Create four holes in the mixture, crack the eggs into each hole, sprinkle with salt and black pepper, and slide the pan into the preheated oven to bake for 6 minutes until the egg whites are set or firm and yolks still runny. Season to taste with salt and pepper, and serve right away with low carb toasts.

NUTRITION

- Kcal: 274
- Fat: 23g
- Net carbs: 4g
- Protein: 13g

 **PREPARATION: 10 MIN**

 **COOKING: 20 MIN**

 **SERVES: 3**

31. BACON AND CHEESE FRITTATA

INGREDIENTS

- 10 slices bacon
- 10 fresh eggs
- 3 tablespoon butter, melted
- ½ cup almond milk
- Salt and black pepper to taste
- 1(½) cups cheddar cheese, shredded
- ¼ cup chopped green onions

DIRECTIONS

1. Preheat the oven to 400°F and grease a baking dish with cooking spray. Cook the bacon in a skillet over medium heat for 6 minutes. Once crispy, remove from the skillet to paper towels and discard grease. Chop into small pieces. Whisk the eggs, butter, milk, salt, and black pepper. Mix in the bacon and pour the mixture into the baking dish.
2. Sprinkle with cheddar cheese and green onions, and bake in the oven for 10 minutes or until the eggs are thoroughly cooked. Remove and cool the frittata for 3 minutes, slice into wedges, and serve warm with a dollop of Greek yogurt.

NUTRITION

- Kcal: 325
- Fat: 28g
- Net carbs: 2g
- Protein: 15g

PREPARATION: 10 MIN

COOKING: 25 MIN

SERVES: 3

32. HAM & EGG BROCCOLI BAKE

INGREDIENTS

- 2 heads broccoli, cut into small florets
- 2 red bell peppers, seeded and chopped
- ¼ cup chopped ham
- 2 teaspoon ghee
- 1 teaspoon dried oregano + extra to garnish
- Salt and black pepper to taste
- 8 fresh eggs

DIRECTIONS

1. Preheat the oven to 425°F.
2. Melt the ghee in a frying pan over medium heat; brown the ham, frequently stirring, about 3 minutes.
3. Arrange the broccoli, bell peppers, and ham on a foil-lined baking sheet in a single layer, toss to combine; season with salt, oregano, and black pepper. Bake for 10 minutes until the vegetables have softened.
4. Remove, create eight indentations with a spoon, and crack an egg into each. Return to the oven and continue to bake for an additional 5 to 7 minutes until the egg whites are firm.
5. Season with salt, black pepper, and extra oregano, share the bake into four plates and serve with strawberry lemonade (optional).

NUTRITION

- Kcal: 344
- Fat: 28g
- Net carbs: 4.2g
- Protein: 11g

 **PREPARATION: 10 MIN**

 **COOKING: 25 MIN**

 **SERVES: 6**

33. CHICKEN, BACON, AND AVOCADO CLOUD SANDWICHES

INGREDIENTS

For cloud bread:
- 3 large eggs
- 4 ounces cream cheese
- ½ tablespoon ground psyllium husk powder
- ½ teaspoon baking powder
- A pinch of salt

To assemble the sandwich:
- 6 slices of bacon, cooked and chopped
- 6 slices pepper Jack cheese
- ½ avocado, sliced
- 1 cup cooked chicken breasts, shredded
- 3 tablespoons mayonnaise

DIRECTIONS

1. Preheat your oven to 300°F.
2. Prepare a baking sheet by lining it with parchment paper.
3. Separate the egg whites and egg yolks, and place into separate bowls.
4. Whisk the egg whites until very stiff. Set aside.
5. Combined egg yolks and cream cheese.
6. Add the psyllium husk powder and baking powder to the egg yolk mixture. Gently fold in.
7. Add the egg whites into the egg mixture and gently fold in.
8. Dollop the mixture onto the prepared baking sheet to create 12 cloud bread. Use a spatula to spread the circles around to form ½-inch thick pieces.
9. Bake for 25 minutes or until the tops are golden brown.
10. Allow the cloud bread to cool completely before serving. Can be refrigerated for up to 3 days or frozen for up to 3 months. If food prepping, place a layer of parchment paper between each bread slice to avoid having them getting stuck together. Simply toast in the oven for 5 minutes when it is time to serve.
11. To assemble sandwiches, place mayonnaise on one side of one cloud bread. Layer with the remaining sandwich ingredients and top with another slice of cloud bread.

NUTRITION

- Calories: 333
- Carbs: 5g
- Fat: 26g
- Protein: 19.9g

PREPARATION: 15 MIN **COOKING: 1H 30 MIN** **SERVES: 12**

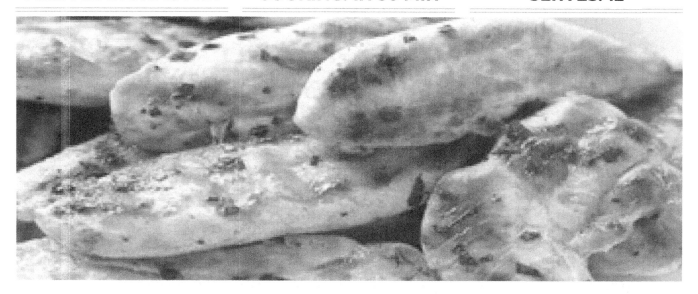

34. ROASTED LEMON CHICKEN SANDWICH

INGREDIENTS

- 1-kilogram whole chicken
- 5 tablespoons butter
- 1 lemon, cut into wedges
- 1 tablespoon garlic powder
- Salt and pepper to taste
- 2 tablespoons mayonnaise
- Keto-friendly bread

DIRECTIONS

1. Preheat the oven to 350°F.
2. Grease a deep baking dish with butter.
3. Ensure that the chicken is patted dry and that the gizzards have been removed.
4. Combine the butter, garlic powder, salt and pepper.
5. Rub the entire chicken with it, including in the cavity.
6. Place the lemon and onion inside the chicken and place the chicken in the prepared baking dish.
7. Bake for about 1(½) hours, depending on the size of the chicken.
8. Baste the chicken often with the drippings. If the drippings begin to dry, add water. The chicken is done when a thermometer, insert it into the thickest part of the thigh reads 165°F or when the clear juices run when the thickest part of the thigh is pierced.
9. Allow the chicken to cool before slicing.
10. To assemble a sandwich, shred some of the breast meat and mix with the mayonnaise. Place the mixture between the two bread slices.
11. To save the chicken, refrigerated for up to 5 days or freeze for up to 1 month.

NUTRITION

- Calories: 214
- Carbs: 1.6g
- Fat: 11.8g
- Protein: 24.4g

PREPARATION: 10 MIN

COOKING: 6 MIN

SERVES: 4

35. KETO-FRIENDLY SKILLET PEPPERONI PIZZA

INGREDIENTS

For crust:
- ½ cup almond flour
- ½ teaspoon baking powder
- 8 large egg whites, whisked into stiff peaks
- Salt and pepper to taste

Toppings:
- 3 tablespoons unsweetened tomato sauce
- ½ cup shredded cheddar cheese
- ½ cup pepperoni

DIRECTIONS

1. Gently incorporate the almond flour into the egg whites. Ensure that no lumps remain.
2. Stir in the remaining crust ingredients.
3. Heat a nonstick skillet over medium heat. Spray with nonstick spray.
4. Pour the batter into the heated skillet to cover the bottom of the skillet.
5. Cover the skillet with a lid and cook the pizza crust to cook for about 4 minutes or until bubbles that appear on the top.
6. Flip the dough and add the toppings, starting with the tomato sauce and ending with the pepperoni
7. Cook the pizza for 2 more minutes.
8. Allow the pizza to cool slightly before serving.
9. Can be stored in the refrigerator for up to 5 days and frozen for up to 1 month.

NUTRITION

- Calories: 175
- Carbs: 1.9g
- Fat: 12g
- Protein: 14.3g

PREPARATION: 5 MIN | **COOKING: 10 MIN** | **SERVES: 4**

36. PESTO SHRIMP WITH ZUCCHINI NOODLES

INGREDIENTS

- 2 cups cauliflower florets, chopped
- ½ cup red bell pepper, chopped
- 1 cup roasted chicken, shredded (Lunch Recipes: Roasted Lemon Chicken Sandwich)
- ¼ cup shredded cheddar cheese
- 1 tablespoon. butter
- 1 tablespoon. sour cream
- Salt and pepper to taste

DIRECTIONS

1. Stir fry the cauliflower and peppers in the butter over medium heat until the veggies are tender.
2. Add the chicken and cook until the chicken is fully heated.
3. Add the remaining ingredients and stir until the cheese is melted.
4. Serve warm.

NUTRITION

- Calories: 144
- Carbs: 4g
- Fat: 8.5g
- Protein: 13.2g

 **PREPARATION: 10**

 **COOKING: 25 MIN**

 **SERVES: 6**

37. CHICKEN SOUP

INGREDIENTS

- 4 cups roasted chicken, shredded (Lunch Recipes: Roasted Lemon Chicken Sandwich)
- 2 tablespoons butter
- 2 celery stalks, chopped
- 1 cup mushrooms, sliced
- 4 cups green cabbage, sliced into strips
- 2 garlic cloves, minced
- 6 cups chicken broth
- 1 carrot, sliced
- Salt and pepper to taste
- 1 tablespoon garlic powder
- 1 tablespoon onion powder

DIRECTIONS

1. Sauté the celery, mushrooms, and garlic in the butter in a pot over medium heat for 4 minutes.
2. Add broth, carrots, garlic powder, onion powder, salt, and pepper.
3. Simmer for 10 minutes or until the vegetables are tender.
4. Add the chicken and cabbage and simmer for another 10 minutes or until the cabbage is tender.
5. Serve warm.
6. Can be refrigerated for up to 3 days or frozen for up to 1 month.

NUTRITION

- Calories: 279
- Carbs: 7.5 g
- Fat: 12.3 g
- Protein: 33.4 g.

PREPARATION: 7 MIN   **COOKING: 10 MIN**   **SERVES: 4**

38. CHICKEN AVOCADO SALAD

INGREDIENTS

- 1 cup roasted chicken, shredded (Lunch Recipes: Roasted Lemon Chicken Sandwich)
- 1 bacon strip, cooked and chopped
- 1/2 medium avocado, chopped
- ¼ cup cheddar cheese, grated
- 1 hard-boiled egg, chopped
- 1 cup romaine lettuce, chopped
- 1 tablespoon. olive oil
- 1 tablespoon. apple cider vinegar
- Salt and pepper to taste

DIRECTIONS

1. Create the dressing by mixing apple cider vinegar, oil, salt, and pepper.
2. Combine all the other ingredients in a mixing bowl.
3. Drizzle with the dressing and toss.
4. Can be refrigerated for up to 3 days.

NUTRITION

- Calories: 220
- Carbs: 2.8g
- Fat: 16.7g
- Protein: 14.8g

PREPARATION: 10 MIN

COOKING: 20 MIN

SERVES: 4

39. EASY MEATBALLS

INGREDIENTS

- 1 ounce ground beef
- 1 egg, beaten
- Salt and pepper to taste
- 1 teaspoon garlic powder
- 1 teaspoon onion powder
- 2 tablespoons butter
- ¼ cup mayonnaise
- ¼ cup pickled jalapenos
- 1 cup cheddar cheese, grated

DIRECTIONS

1. Combine the cheese, mayonnaise, pickled jalapenos, salt, pepper, garlic powder, and onion powder in a large mixing bowl.
2. Add the beef and egg and combine using clean hands.
3. Form large meatballs. Makes about 12.
4. Fry the meatballs in the butter over medium heat for about 4 minutes on each side or until golden brown.
5. Serve warm with a keto-friendly side.
6. The meatball mixture can also be used to make a meatloaf. Just preheat your oven to 400°F, press the mixture into a loaf pan and bake for about 30 minutes or until the top is golden brown.
7. Can be refrigerated for up to 5 days or frozen for up to 3 months.

NUTRITION

- Calories: 454
- Carbs: 5g
- Fat: 28.2g
- Protein: 43.2g

PREPARATION: 10 MIN

COOKING: 40 MIN

SERVES: 8

40. CHICKEN CASSEROLE

INGREDIENTS

- 1 ounce boneless chicken breasts, cut into 1" cubes
- 2 tablespoons butter
- 4 tablespoons green pesto
- 1 cup heavy whipping cream
- ¼ cup green bell peppers, diced
- 1 cup feta cheese, diced
- 1 garlic clove, minced
- Salt and pepper to taste

DIRECTIONS

1. Preheat your oven to 400°F.
2. Season the chicken with salt and pepper, then batch fry in the butter until golden brown.
3. Place the fried chicken pieces in a baking dish. Add the feta cheese, garlic, and bell peppers.
4. Combine the pesto and heavy cream in a bowl. Pour on top of the chicken mixture and spread with a spatula.
5. Bake for 30 minutes or until the casserole is light brown around the edges.
6. Serve warm.
7. Can be refrigerated for up to 5 days and frozen for 2 weeks.

NUTRITION

- Calories: 294
- Carbs: 1.7g
- Fat: 22.7g
- Protein: 20.1g

PREPARATION: 10 MIN

COOKING: 30 MIN

SERVES: 4

41. LEMON BAKED SALMON

INGREDIENTS

- 1 pound salmon
- 1 tablespoon olive oil
- Salt and pepper to taste
- 1 tablespoon butter
- 1 lemon, thinly sliced
- 1 tablespoon lemon juice

DIRECTIONS

1. Preheat your oven to 400°F.
2. Grease a baking dish with the olive oil and place the salmon skin-side down.
3. Season the salmon with salt and pepper, then top with the lemon slices.
4. Slice half the butter and place over the salmon.
5. Bake for 20 minutes or until the salmon flakes easily.
6. Melt the remaining butter in a saucepan. When it starts to bubble, remove from heat and allow to cool before adding the lemon juice.
7. Drizzle the lemon butter over the salmon and Serve warm.

NUTRITION

- Calories: 211
- Carbs: 1.5g
- Fat: 13.5g
- Protein: 22.2g

PREPARATION: 10 MIN

COOKING: 5 MIN

SERVES: 8

42. CAULIFLOWER MASH

INGREDIENTS

- 4 cups cauliflower florets, chopped
- 1 cup grated parmesan cheese
- 6 tablespoons butter
- ½ lemon, juice and zest
- Salt and pepper to taste

DIRECTIONS

1. Boil the cauliflower in lightly salted water over high heat for 5 minutes or until the florets are tender but still firm.
2. Strain the cauliflower in a colander and add the cauliflower to a food processor
3. Add the remaining ingredients and pulse the mixture to a smooth and creamy consistency
4. Serve with protein like salmon, chicken or meatballs.
5. Can be refrigerated for up to 3 days.

NUTRITION

- Calories: 101
- Carbs: 3.1g
- Fat: 9.5g
- Protein: 2.2g

PREPARATION: 10 MIN

COOKING: 4 MIN

SERVES: 8

43. BAKED SALMON

INGREDIENTS

- Cooking spray
- 3 cloves garlic, minced
- ¼ cup butter
- 1 teaspoon lemon zest
- 2 tablespoons lemon juice
- 4 salmon fillets
- Salt and pepper to taste
- 2 tablespoons parsley, chopped

DIRECTIONS

1. Preheat your oven to 425°F.
2. Grease the pan with cooking spray.
3. In a bowl, mix the garlic, butter, and lemon zest, and lemon juice.
4. Sprinkle salt and pepper on salmon fillets.
5. Drizzle with the lemon butter sauce.
6. Bake in the oven for 12 minutes.
7. Garnish with parsley before serving.

NUTRITION

- Calories: 345
- Total Fat: 22.7g
- Saturated Fat: 8.9g
- Cholesterol: 109mg
- Sodium: 163mg
- Total carbohydrate: 1.2g
- Dietary Fiber: 0.2g
- Total sugars: 0.2g
- Protein: 34.9g
- Potassium: 718mg

PREPARATION: 10 MIN

COOKING: 10 MIN

SERVES: 8

44. TUNA PATTIES

INGREDIENTS

- 20 ounces canned tuna flakes
- ¼ cup almond flour
- 1 egg, beaten
- 2 tablespoons fresh dill, chopped
- 2 stalks green onion, chopped
- Salt and pepper to taste
- 1 tablespoon lemon zest
- ¼ cup mayonnaise
- 1 tablespoon lemon juice
- 2 tablespoons avocado oil

DIRECTIONS

1. Combine all the ingredients except avocado oil, lemon juice and avocado oil in a large bowl.
2. Form 8 patties from the mixture.
3. In a pan over medium heat, add the oil.
4. Once the oil starts to sizzle, cook the tuna patties for 3 to 4 minutes per side.
5. Drain each patty on a paper towel.
6. Spread mayo on top and drizzle with lemon juice before serving.

NUTRITION

- Calories: 101
- Total fat: 4.9g
- Saturated fat: 1.2g
- Cholesterol: 47mg
- Sodium: 243mg
- Total carbohydrate: 3.1g
- Dietary fiber: 0.5g
- Total sugars: 0.7g
- Protein: 12.3g
- Potassium: 60mg

 **PREPARATION: 20 MIN**

 **COOKING: 10 MIN**

 SERVES: 6

45. GRILLED MAHI WITH LEMON BUTTER SAUCE

INGREDIENTS

- 6 Mahi fillets
- Salt and pepper to taste
- 2 tablespoons olive oil
- 6 tablespoons butter
- ¼ onion, minced
- ½ teaspoon garlic, minced
- ¼ cup chicken stock
- 1 tablespoon lemon juice

DIRECTIONS

1. Preheat your grill to medium heat.
2. Season fish fillets with salt and pepper.
3. Coat both sides with olive oil.
4. Grill for 3 to 4 minutes per side.
5. Place fish on a serving platter.
6. In a pan over medium heat, add the butter and let it melt.
7. Add the onion and sauté for 2 minutes.
8. Add the garlic and cook for 30 seconds.
9. Pour in the chicken stock.
10. Simmer until the stock has been reduced to half.
11. Add the lemon juice.
12. Pour the sauce over the grilled fish fillets.

NUTRITION

- Calories: 234
- Total fat: 17.2g
- Saturated fat: 8.3g
- Cholesterol: 117mg
- Sodium: 242mg
- Total carbohydrate: 0.6g
- Dietary fiber: 0.1g
- Total sugars: 0.3g
- Protein: 19.1g
- Potassium: 385mg

PREPARATION: 15 MIN

COOKING: 10 MIN

SERVES: 6

46. SHRIMP SCAMPI

INGREDIENTS

- 2 tablespoons olive oil
- 2 tablespoons butter
- 1 tablespoon garlic, minced
- ½ cup dry white wine
- ¼ teaspoon red pepper flakes
- Salt and pepper to taste
- 2 pounds large shrimp, peeled and deveined
- ¼ cup fresh parsley, chopped
- 1 teaspoon lemon zest
- 2 tablespoons lemon juice
- 3 cups spaghetti squash, cooked

DIRECTIONS

1. In a pan over medium heat, add the oil and butter.
2. Cook the garlic for 2 minutes.
3. Pour in the wine.
4. Add the red pepper flakes, salt and pepper.
5. Cook for 2 minutes.
6. Add the shrimp.
7. Cook for 2 to 3 minutes.
8. Remove from the stove.
9. Add the parsley, lemon zest and lemon juice.
10. Serve on top of spaghetti squash.

NUTRITION

- Calories: 232
- Total fat: 8.9g
- Saturated fat: 3.2g
- Cholesterol: 226mg
- Sodium: 229mg
- Total carbohydrate: 7.6g
- Dietary fiber: 0.2g
- Total sugars: 0.3g
- Protein: 28.9g
- Potassium: 104mg

PREPARATION: 10 MIN

COOKING: 25 MIN

SERVES: 3

47. ITALIAN SAUSAGE STACKS

INGREDIENTS

- 6 Italian sausage patties
- 4 tablespoon olive oil
- 2 ripe avocados, pitted
- 2 teaspoon fresh lime juice
- Salt and black pepper to taste
- 6 fresh eggs
- Red pepper flakes to garnish

DIRECTIONS

1. In a skillet, warm the oil over medium heat and fry the sausage patties about 8 minutes until lightly browned and firm. Remove the patties to a plate.
2. Spoon the avocado into a bowl, mash with the lime juice, and season with salt and black pepper. Spread the mash on the sausages.
3. Boil 3 cups of water in a wide pan over high heat, and reduce to simmer (don't boil).
4. Crack each egg into a small bowl and gently put the egg into the simmering water; poach for 2 to 3 minutes. Use a perforated spoon to remove from the water on a paper towel to dry. Repeat with the other 5 eggs. Top each stack with a poached egg, sprinkle with chili flakes, salt, black pepper, and chives. Serve with turnip wedges.

NUTRITION

- Kcal: 378
- Fat: 23g
- Net carbs: 5g
- Protein: 16g

 **PREPARATION: 10 MIN**  **COOKING: 25 MIN** **SERVES: 3**

48. SMOKED SALMON ROLLS WITH DILL CREAM CHEESE

INGREDIENTS

- 3 tablespoon cream cheese, softened
- 1 small lemon, zested and juiced
- 3 teaspoon chopped fresh dill
- Salt and black pepper to taste
- 3 (7-inch) low carb tortillas
- 6 slices smoked salmon

DIRECTIONS

1. In a bowl, mix the cream cheese, lemon juice, zest, dill, salt, and black pepper.
2. Lay each tortilla on a plastic wrap (just wide enough to cover the tortilla), spread with cream cheese mixture, and top each (one) with two salmon slices. Roll up the tortillas and secure both ends by twisting.
3. Refrigerate for 2 hours, remove plastic, cut off both ends of each wrap, and cut wraps into wheels.

NUTRITION

- Kcal: 250
- Fat: 16g
- Net carbs: 7g
- Protein: 18g

 **PREPARATION: 10 MIN**
 **COOKING: 35 MIN**
 **SERVES: 4**

49. SPINACH CHICKEN CHEESY BAKE

INGREDIENTS

- 1 lb. chicken breasts
- 1 tsp mixed spice seasoning
- Pink salt and black pepper to taste
- 2 loose cups baby spinach
- 3 tsp olive oil
- 4 oz cream cheese
- 1 ¼ cups mozzarella cheese, grated
- 4 tbsp water

DIRECTIONS

1. Preheat oven to 370°F. Season chicken with spice mix, salt, and black pepper. Pat with your hands to have the seasoning stick on the chicken. Put in the casserole dish and layer spinach over the chicken. Mix the oil with cream cheese, mozzarella, salt, and pepper and stir in water a tablespoon at a time.
2. Pour the mixture over the chicken and cover the casserole dish with aluminum foil. Bake for 20 minutes. Remove the foil and continue cooking for 15 minutes until a nice golden-brown color is formed on top. Take out and allow sitting for 5 minutes. Serve warm with braised asparagus.

NUTRITION

- Calories: 340
- Fat: 30.2g
- Net Carbs: 3.1g
- Protein: 15g

PREPARATION: 5 MIN	**COOKING: 20 MIN**	**SERVES: 4**

50. CILANTRO CHICKEN BREASTS WITH MAYO-AVOCADO SAUCE

INGREDIENTS

Mayo-avocado sauce
- 1 avocado, pitted
- ½ cup mayonnaise
- Salt to taste

Chicken
- 2 tbsp ghee
- 4 chicken breasts
- Pink salt and black pepper to taste
- 2 tbsp fresh cilantro, chopped
- ½ cup chicken broth

DIRECTIONS

1. Spoon the avocado into a bowl and mash with a fork. Add in mayonnaise and salt and stir until a smooth sauce is derived. Pour sauce into a jar and refrigerate. Melt the ghee in a large skillet over medium heat. Season chicken with salt and pepper and fry for 4 minutes on each side until golden brown. Remove.
2. Pour the broth in the same skillet and add the cilantro. Bring to simmer covered for 3 minutes and return the chicken. Cover and cook on low heat for 5 minutes until the liquid has reduced and the chicken is fragrant. Place the chicken only into serving plates and spoon the mayo-avocado sauce over. Serve.

NUTRITION

- Calories: 398
- Fat: 32g
- Net Carbs: 4g
- Protein: 24g

PREPARATION: 10 MIN **COOKING: 1H 20** **SERVES: 4**

51. CHICKEN DRUMSTICKS IN TOMATO SAUCE

INGREDIENTS

- 8 chicken drumsticks
- 2 tbsp olive oil
- 1 medium white onion, chopped
- 2 medium turnips, peeled and diced
- 1 medium carrot, chopped
- 2 green bell peppers, cut into chunks
- 2 cloves garlic, minced
- ¼ cup coconut flour
- 1 cup chicken broth
- 1 (28 oz) can sugar-free tomato sauce
- 2 tbsp dried Italian herbs
- Salt and black pepper to taste

DIRECTIONS

1. Preheat oven to 400°F. Heat the olive oil in a skillet over medium heat. Season the drumsticks with salt and pepper and fry for 10 minutes on all sides until brown. Remove to a baking dish. Sauté the onion, turnips, bell peppers, carrot, and garlic in the same oil for 10 minutes with continuous stirring.
2. In a bowl, combine the broth, coconut flour, tomato paste, and Italian herbs together and pour it over the vegetables in the skillet. Stir and cook for 4 minutes until thickened. Pour the mixture over the chicken in the baking dish. Bake for around 1 hour. Remove from the oven and serve with steamed cauliflower rice.

NUTRITION

- Calories: 515
- Fat: 34.2g
- Net Carbs: 7.3g
- Protein: 50.8g

PREPARATION: 10 MIN

COOKING: 55 MIN

SERVES: 6

52. ROASTED CHICKEN BREASTS WITH CAPERS

INGREDIENTS

- 2 medium lemons, sliced
- 3 chicken breasts, halved
- Salt and black pepper to taste
- ¼ cup almond flour
- 3 tbsp olive oil
- 2 tbsp capers, rinsed
- 1 ¼ cups chicken broth
- 2 tbsp fresh parsley, chopped
- 1 tbsp butter

DIRECTIONS

1. Preheat oven to 350°F.
2. Line a baking sheet with parchment paper. Lay the lemon slices on the baking sheet and drizzle with some olive oil. Roast for 25 minutes until the lemon rinds brown.
3. Cover the chicken with plastic wrap, place them on a flat surface, and gently pound with the rolling pin to flatten to about ½-inch thickness. Remove the plastic wraps and season with salt and pepper. Dredge the chicken in the almond flour on each side, and shake off any excess flour. Set aside.
4. Heat the remaining olive oil in a skillet over medium heat. Fry the chicken on both sides until golden brown, about 8 minutes. Pour in the broth and let it boil until it becomes thick in consistency, 12 minutes.
5. Stir in the capers, butter, and roasted lemons and simmer on low heat for 10 minutes. Turn the heat off. Pour the sauce over the chicken and garnish it with parsley to serve.

NUTRITION

- Calories: 430
- Fat: 23g
- Net Carb:s 3g
- Protein: 33g

PREPARATION: 10 MIN

COOKING: 15 MIN

SERVES: 4

53. SWEET GARLIC CHICKEN SKEWERS

INGREDIENTS

Skewers
- 3 tbsp soy sauce
- 1 tbsp ginger-garlic paste
- 2 tbsp swerve brown sugar
- 1 tsp chili pepper
- 2 tbsp olive oil
- 1 lb. chicken breasts, cut into cubes

Dressing
- ½ cup tahini
- ½ tsp garlic powder
- Pink salt to taste

DIRECTIONS

1. In a bowl, whisk soy sauce, ginger-garlic paste, swerve brown sugar, chili pepper, and olive oil. Put the chicken in a zipper bag. Pour in the marinade, seal, and shake to coat. Marinate in the fridge for 2 hours.
2. Preheat grill to 400°F. Thread the chicken on skewers. Cook for 10 minutes in total with three to four turnings until golden brown; remove to a plate. Mix the tahini, garlic powder, salt, and ¼ cup of warm water in a bowl. Pour into serving jars. Serve the chicken skewers and tahini dressing with cauliflower rice.

NUTRITION

- Calories: 225
- Fat: 17.4g
- Net Carbs: 2g
- Protein: 15g

PREPARATION: 10 MIN	**COOKING: 30 MIN**	**SERVES: 4**

54. CHICKEN IN WHITE WINE SAUCE

INGREDIENTS

- 1 ½ chicken thighs
- Salt and black pepper to taste
- 2 shallots, chopped
- 2 tbsp canola oil
- 4 pancetta strips, chopped
- 2 garlic cloves, minced
- 10 oz white mushrooms, halved
- 1 cup white wine
- 1 cup whipping cream

DIRECTIONS

1. Warm the canola oil in pan over medium heat. Cook the pancetta for 3 minutes. Add in the chicken, sprinkle with pepper and salt, and cook until brown, about 5 minutes. Remove to a plate. In the same pan, sauté shallots, mushrooms, and garlic for 6 minutes. Return the pancetta and chicken to the pan.
2. Stir in the white wine and 1 cup of water and bring to a boil. Reduce the heat and simmer for 20 minutes. Pour in the whipping cream and warm without boiling. Serve with steamed asparagus.

NUTRITION

- Calories: 345
- Fat: 12g
- Net Carbs: 4g
- Protein: 24g

PREPARATION: 10 MIN

COOKING: 50 MIN

SERVES: 4

55. STUFFED CHICKEN BREASTS WITH CUCUMBER NOODLE SALAD

INGREDIENTS

Chicken
- 4 chicken breasts
- 1 cup baby spinach
- ¼ cup goat cheese
- ¼ cup cheddar cheese, shredded
- 4 tbsp butter, melted
- Salt and black pepper to taste
- Tomato sauce
- 1 tbsp butter
- 1 shallot, chopped
- 2 garlic cloves, chopped
- ½ tbsp liquid stevia
- 2 tbsp tomato paste
- 14 oz canned crushed tomatoes
- Salt and black pepper to taste
- 1 tsp dried basil
- 1 tsp dried oregano

Salad
- 2 cucumbers, spiralized
- 2 tbsp olive oil
- 1 tbsp white wine vinegar

DIRECTIONS

1. Preheat oven to 400°F. Place a pan over medium heat. Warm 2 tbsp of butter and sauté spinach until it shrinks. Season with salt and pepper. Transfer to a bowl containing goat cheese, stir, and set aside.
2. Cut the chicken breasts lengthwise and stuff with the cheese mixture. Set into a baking dish. On top, spread the cheddar cheese and add 2 tbsp of butter. Bake until cooked through for 25-30 minutes.
3. Warm 1 tbsp of the butter in a pan over medium heat. Add in garlic and shallot and cook for 3 minutes until soft. Stir in herbs, tomato paste, stevia, tomatoes, salt, and pepper and cook for 15 minutes.
4. Arrange the cucumbers on a serving platter, season with salt, pepper, olive oil, and vinegar. Top with the chicken and pour over the sauce. Serve.

NUTRITION

- Calories: 453
- Fat: 31g
- Net Carbs: 6g
- Protein: 43g

PREPARATION: 5 MIN   **COOKING: 25 MIN**   **SERVES: 6**

56. PARMESAN WINGS WITH YOGURT SAUCE

INGREDIENTS

- 1 cup Greek-style yogurt
- 2 tbsp extra-virgin olive oil
- 1 tbsp fresh dill, chopped
- 2 lb. chicken wings
- Salt and black pepper to taste
- ½ cup butter, melted
- ½ cup hot sauce
- ¼ cup Parmesan cheese, grated

DIRECTIONS

1. Preheat oven to 400°F. Mix yogurt, olive oil, dill, salt, and black pepper in a bowl. Chill while making the chicken. Season wings with salt and pepper. Line them on a baking sheet and grease them with cooking spray.
2. Bake for 20 minutes until golden brown. Mix butter, hot sauce, and Parmesan cheese in a bowl. Toss chicken in the sauce to evenly coat and plate. Serve with yogurt dipping sauce.

NUTRITION

- Calories: 452,
- Fat: 36.4g
- Net Carbs: 4g
- Protein: 24g

PREPARATION: 10 MIN   **COOKING: 30 MIN**   **SERVES: 4**

57. CREAMY STUFFED CHICKEN WITH PARMA HAM

INGREDIENTS

- 4 chicken breasts
- 2 tbsp olive oil
- 2 cloves garlic, minced
- 2 shallots, finely chopped
- 1 tsp dried mixed herbs
- 8 slices Parma ham
- 4 oz cream cheese, softened
- 1 lemon, zested
- Salt to taste

DIRECTIONS

1. Preheat oven to 350°F. Heat the oil in a skillet over medium heat. Sauté garlic and shallots for 3 minutes. Stir the cream cheese, mixed herbs, salt, and lemon zest for 2 minutes. Remove and let cool.
2. Score a pocket in each chicken breast, fill the holes with the cheese mixture, and cover with the cut-out chicken. Wrap each breast with 2 ham slices and secure the ends with a toothpick. Lay the chicken parcels on a greased baking sheet. Bake for 20 minutes. Remove and let it rest for 4 minutes. Serve.

NUTRITION

- Calories: 485
- Fat: 35g
- Net Carbs: 2g
- Protein: 26g

PREPARATION: 10 MIN

COOKING: 40 MIN

SERVES: 6

58. CHICKEN CAULIFLOWER BAKE

INGREDIENTS

- 3 cups cubed leftover chicken
- 3 cups spinach
- 2 cauliflower heads, cut into florets
- 3 eggs, lightly beaten
- 2 cups grated sharp cheddar cheese
- 1 cup pork rinds, crushed
- ½ cup unsweetened almond milk
- 3 tbsp olive oil
- 3 cloves garlic, minced

DIRECTIONS

1. Preheat oven to 350°F. Pour the cauliflower florets and 3 cups water in a pot over medium heat and bring to a boil. Cover and steam the cauliflower florets for 8 minutes. Drain through a colander and set aside. Combine the cheddar cheese and pork rinds in a large bowl and mix in the chicken. Set aside.
2. Heat the olive oil in a skillet and cook the garlic and spinach until the spinach has wilted, about 5 minutes. Add the spinach mixture and cauliflower florets to the chicken bowl. Add in the eggs and almond milk, mix, and transfer everything to a greased baking dish. Layer the top of the ingredients.
3. Place the dish in the oven and bake for 30 minutes. By this time, the edges and top must have browned nicely. Remove the chicken from the oven, let rest for 5 minutes, and serve.

NUTRITION

- Calories: 390
- Fat: 27g
- Net Carbs: 3g
- Protein: 22g

8. DINNER RECIPES

PREPARATION: 20 MIN  **COOKING: 15 MIN**   **SERVES: 4**

59. TURMERIC CHICKEN AND CABBAGE SALAD WITH LEMON AND HONEY

INGREDIENTS

For the chicken:
- 1 teaspoon of clarified butter or 1 tablespoon of coconut oil
- ½ medium brown onion, diced
- 250–300 grams/9 ounces minced chicken meat or diced chicken legs
- 1 large garlic clove, diced
- 1 teaspoon turmeric powder
- 1 teaspoon lime zest
- ½ lime juice
- ½ teaspoon salt + pepper

For the salad:
- 6 stalks of broccoli or 2 cups of broccoli flowers
- 2 tablespoons of pumpkin seeds (seeds)
- 3 large cabbage leaves, stems removed and chopped
- ½ sliced avocado
- A handful of fresh coriander leaves, chopped
- A handful of fresh parsley leaves, chopped

For the dressing:
- 3 tablespoons lime juice
- 1 small garlic clove, diced or grated
- 3 tablespoons of virgin olive oil (I used 1 tablespoon of avocado oil and 2 tablespoons of EVO)
- 1 teaspoon raw honey
- ½ teaspoon whole or Dijon mustard
- ½ teaspoon sea salt with pepper

DIRECTIONS

1. Heat the coconut oil in a pan. Add the onion and sauté over medium heat for 4–5 minutes, until golden brown. Add the minced chicken and garlic and stir 2–3 minutes over medium-high heat, separating.
2. Add your turmeric, lime zest, lime juice, salt, and pepper, and cook, stirring consistently, for another 3–4 minutes. Set the ground beef aside.
3. While your chicken is cooking, put a small saucepan of water to the boil. Add your broccoli and cook for 2 minutes. Rinse with cold water and cut into 3–4 pieces each.
4. Add the pumpkin seeds to the chicken pan and toast over medium heat for 2 minutes, frequently stirring to avoid burning. Season with a little salt. Set aside. Raw pumpkin seeds are also good to use.
5. Put the chopped cabbage in a salad bowl and pour it over the dressing. Using your hands, mix, and massage the cabbage with the dressing. This will soften the cabbage, a bit like citrus juice with fish or beef Carpaccio: it "cooks" it a little.
6. Finally, mix the cooked chicken, broccoli, fresh herbs, pumpkin seeds, and avocado slices.

NUTRITION

- Calories: 232
- Fat: 11g
- Fiber: 9g
- Carbs: 8g
- Protein: 14g

PREPARATION: 5 MIN

COOKING: 15 MIN

SERVES: 1-2

60. EGG-CRUST PIZZA

INGREDIENTS

- ¼ teaspoon dried oregano to taste
- ½ teaspoon spike seasoning to taste
- 1 ounce of mozzarella, chopped into small cubes
- 6–8 sliced thinly black olives
- 6 slices of turkey pepperoni, sliced into half
- 4–5 thinly sliced small grape tomatoes
- 2 eggs, beaten well
- 1–2 teaspoons of olive oil

DIRECTIONS

1. Preheat the broiler in an oven, then in a small bowl, beat well the eggs. Cut the pepperoni and tomatoes in slices, then cut the mozzarella cheese into cubes.
2. Put some olive oil in a skillet over medium heat, then heat the pan for around one minute until it begins to get hot. Add in eggs and season with oregano and spike seasoning, then cook for around 2 minutes until the eggs begin to set at the bottom.
3. Drizzle half of the mozzarella, olives, pepperoni and tomatoes on the eggs followed by another layer of the remaining half of the above ingredients. Ensure that there is a lot of cheese on the topmost layers. Cover the skillet using a lid and cook until the cheese begins to melt and the eggs are set, for around 3–4 minutes.
4. Place the pan under the preheated broiler and cook until the top has browned and the cheese has melted nicely for around 2–3 minutes. Serve immediately.

NUTRITION

- Calories: 363
- Fats: 24.1g
- Carbs: 20.8g
- Proteins: 19.25g

PREPARATION: 10 MIN

COOKING: 5 MIN

SERVES: 1

61. CHICKEN BROCCOLI DINNER

INGREDIENTS

- 1 roasted chicken leg (Lunch Recipes: Roasted Lemon Chicken Sandwich)
- ½ cup broccoli florets
- ½ tablespoon unsalted butter softened
- 2 garlic cloves, minced
- Salt and pepper to taste

DIRECTIONS

1. Boil the broccoli in lightly salted water for 5 minutes. Drain the water from the pot and keep the broccoli in the pot. Keep the lid on to keep the broccoli warm.
2. Mix all the butter, garlic, salt, and pepper in a small bowl to create garlic butter.
3. Place the chicken, broccoli, and garlic butter.

NUTRITION

- Calories: 257
- Carbs: 5.1g
- Fat: 14g
- Protein: 27.4g

 **PREPARATION: 10 MIN**  **COOKING: 15 MIN**  **SERVES: 8**

62. CHICKEN BACON BURGER

INGREDIENTS

- 4 chicken breasts
- 4 slices bacon
- 1/4 medium onion
- 2 cloves of garlic
- 1/4 cup (60 ml) avocado oil, to cook with

DIRECTIONS

1. Food process the chicken, bacon, onion, and garlic and form 8 patties. You need to do this in batches.
2. Fry patties in the avocado oil in batches. Make sure burgers are fully cooked.
3. Serve with guacamole

NUTRITION

- Calories: 319
- Fat: 24 g
- NetCarbohydrates: 1 g
- Protein: 25 g

PREPARATION: 10 MIN **COOKING: 15 MIN** **SERVES: 2**

63. BASIL CHICKEN SAUTÉ

INGREDIENTS

- 1 chicken breast, minced or chopped very small
- 2 cloves of garlic, minced
- 1 chili pepper, diced (optional)
- 1 cup basil leaves, finely chopped
- 1 Tablespoon tamari sauce
- 2 Tablespoons avocado or coconut oil to cook in
- Salt, to taste

DIRECTIONS

1. Add oil to a frying pan and sauté the garlic and pepper.
2. Then add in the minced chicken and sauté until the chicken is cooked.
3. Add the tamari sauce and salt to taste. Add in the basil leaves and mix them in.

NUTRITION

- Calories: 320
- Fat: 24 g
- NetCarbohydrates: 2 g
- Protein: 24 g

PREPARATION: 10 MIN **COOKING: 5H** **SERVES: 4**

64. SLOW COOKER JERK CHICKEN

INGREDIENTS

- chicken drumsticks and 8 chicken wings
- 4 teaspoons (20 g) salt
- 4 teaspoons (9 g) paprika
- 1 teaspoon (2 g) cayenne pepper
- 2 teaspoons (5 g) onion powder
- 2 teaspoons (3 g) dried thyme
- 2 teaspoons (4 g) white pepper
- 2 teaspoons (6 g) garlic powder
- 1 teaspoon (2 g) black pepper

DIRECTIONS

1. Put all the spices in a bowl, then mix to make a rub for the chicken.
2. Wash the chicken meat in cold water briefly. Place the washed chicken meat into the bowl with the rub, and rub the spices onto the meat thoroughly, including under the skin.
3. Place each piece of chicken covered with the spices into the slow cooker (no liquid required).
4. Set the slow cooker on medium heat, and cook for 5 hours or until the chicken meat falls off the bone.

NUTRITION

- Calories: 480
- Fat: 30 g
- NetCarbohydrates: 4 g
- Protein: 45 g

PREPARATION: 10 MIN   **COOKING: 30 MIN**   **SERVES: 2**

65. PULLED BUFFALO CHICKEN SALAD WITH BLUE CHEESE

INGREDIENTS

- 2 boneless, skinless free-range chicken breasts
- 4 uncured center-cut bacon strips
- ¼ cup Buffalo Sauce
- 4 cups chopped romaine lettuce, divided
- ½ cup blue cheese dressing, divided
- ½ cup crumbled organic blue cheese, divided
- ¼ cup chopped red onion, divided

DIRECTIONS

1. Place a large pot of water to a boil over high heat.
2. Put the chicken breasts in the water, lower the heat then simmer the breasts until their internal temperature reaches 180°F, about 30 minutes.
3. Take the chicken to a bowl and let it cool for about 10 minutes.
4. On the other hand, crisp the bacon strips in a skillet over medium heat, about 3 minutes per side. Drain the bacon on a paper towel.
5. Shred the chicken using a fork and toss it with the buffalo sauce.
6. Divide the lettuce into 2 bowls. Top each with half of the pulled chicken, half of the blue cheese dressing, blue cheese crumbles, and chopped red onion. Crumble the bacon over the salads and serve.

NUTRITION

- Calories: 843
- Total Fat: 65g
- Saturated Fat: 14g
- Protein: 59g
- Cholesterol: 156mg
- Carbohydrates: 6g
- Fiber: 1g
- Net Carbs: 5g

PREPARATION: 10 MIN

COOKING: 20 MIN

SERVES: 4

66. LAMB BURGERS WITH TZATZIKI

INGREDIENTS

- 1 lb. grass-fed lamb
- ¼ cup chives finely chopped green onion or red onion if desired
- 1 tablespoon chopped fresh dill
- ½ tsp dried oregano or about 1 tablespoon freshly chopped
- 1 tablespoon finely chopped fresh mint
- A pinch chopped red pepper
- Fine-grained sea salt
- 1 tablespoon water
- 2 tsp olive oil to grease the pan

For the tzatziki
- 1 can coconut milk with all the cooled fat and 1 tablespoon the discarded liquid portion **
- 3 cloves garlic
- 1 peeled cucumber without seeds, roughly sliced
- 1 tablespoon freshly squeezed lemon juice
- 2 tablespoon chopped fresh dill
- 3/4 tsp fine grain sea salt
- Black pepper to taste

DIRECTIONS

1. Place the garlic, cucumber, and lemon juice in the food processor and press until finely chopped. Add the coconut cream, dill, salt, and pepper, and mix until well blended.
2. Put it in a jar with a lid and keep it in the refrigerator until it is served. The flavors become more intense over time when they cool in the fridge.
3. Thoroughly mix the ground lamb in a bowl with the chives or red onion, dill, oregano, mint, red pepper, and water.
4. Sprinkle the mixture with fine-grained sea salt and form 4 patties of the same size.
5. Heat a large cast-iron skillet over medium heat and brush with a small amount of olive oil. Lightly sprinkle the pan with fine-grain sea salt.
6. Bring the patties into the pan and cook on each side for about 4 min, adjusting the heat to prevent the outside from becoming too brown. Alternatively, you can grill the burgers.
7. Remove from the pan and cover with tzatziki sauce.

NUTRITION

- Calories: 363
- Protein: 35.33 g
- Fat: 22.14 g
- Carbohydrates: 6.83 g

PREPARATION: 5 MIN

COOKING: 15 MIN

SERVES: 6

67. LAMB SLIDERS

INGREDIENTS

- 1 lb. minced lamb or half veal, half lamb
- ½ sliced onion
- 2 garlic cloves minced
- 1 tablespoon dried dill
- 1 tsp salt
- ½ tsp black pepper

DIRECTIONS

1. Blend the ingredients gently in a large bowl until well combined. Overworking the meat will cause it to be tough.
2. Form the meat into burgers.
3. Grill or fry in a pan on medium-high heat until cooked through, 4-5 min per side. If preparing in a pan, to sear both sides quickly, then throw the burgers in a 350° F oven for 10 min to finish cooking through.
4. Serve with Tzatziki for dipping!

NUTRITION

- Calories: 207
- Protein: 22.68 g
- Fat: 11.89 g
- Carbohydrates: 1.17 g

PREPARATION: 30 MIN **COOKING: 30 MIN** **SERVES: 2**

68. NO-PASTRY BEEF WELLINGTON

INGREDIENTS

For the duxelles:
- 3 large button mushrooms
- 1 Tablespoon onions, chopped
- 1 teaspoon garlic powder
- 1/2 teaspoon salt
- 2 Tablespoons olive oil

Other ingredients:
- 1 9-ounce filet mignon
- 8 thin slices prosciutto
- 1 tablespoon yellow mustard
- 1/2 Tablespoon salt
- 2 Tablespoons olive oil to cook in

DIRECTIONS

1. Set the oven to 400°F
2. Make the duxelles by mixing the mushrooms, onions, garlic powder, salt, and olive oil until pureed.
3. Warm the mixture in a pan for 10 minutes on medium heat.
4. Put a large piece of cling-film onto the counter and place the slices of prosciutto per side (overlapping slightly) to form a rectangular layer.
5. Spread the duxelles on the prosciutto layer.
6. Dust the 1 tbsp of salt over the filet mignon.
7. Pan-sear the filet mignon in 2 tablespoon of olive oil.
8. Spread the 1 tablespoon of mustard on the seared filet mignon, then put in the middle of the prosciutto and duxelles layer.
9. Using the cling-film, wrap the prosciutto around the filet mignon. Then wrap the cling-film around the package to secure it. Use a second piece of cling-film to pull the prosciutto-wrapped package tighter together. Refrigerate for 15 minutes.
10. Take off the cling-film from the refrigerated prosciutto-wrapped beef and place beef on a greased baking tray.
11. Bake for at least 20-25 minutes (it should be pink when you cut into it).
12. To serve, carefully cut the Beef Wellington in half.

NUTRITION

- Calories: 580
- Fat: 50 g
- NetCarbohydrates: 2 g
- Protein: 30 g

PREPARATION: 15 MIN

COOKING: 45 MIN

SERVES: 2

69. LAMB SOUVLAKI

INGREDIENTS

- 2 lbs. Fat-free lamb, cut into 1-inch pieces
- 2 lemon juice
- 3 tablespoon olive oil
- ½ tsp salt
- ½ tsp freshly ground pepper
- 1 tablespoon dried oregano
- garlic cloves, finely chopped
- 1 medium onion, thinly sliced

DIRECTIONS

1. Combine olive oil, lemon juice, salt, pepper, oregano, garlic, and onion in a large bowl. Place the slices of meat in the pan and mix so that the meat is completely covered with marinade. Cover and let cool for a minimum of 2 hours and a maximum of 24 hours. Bring chicken on metal or bamboo skewers.
2. Roast the skewer on all sides until golden.
3. Serve with pita bread.

NUTRITION

- Calories: 1396
- Protein: 114.74 g
- Fat: 99.7 g
- Carbohydrates: 4.23 g

PREPARATION: 15 MIN **COOKING: 50 MIN** **SERVES: 4**

70. LAMB SAAGWALA

INGREDIENTS

- 2 to 3 lb. of Fat-free lamb, cut into 1-inch cubes
- 4 tablespoon, divided
- 2 dried red peppers
- 1-inch cinnamon stick
- 4 green cardamom pods
- 1 tablespoon coriander seeds
- 2 tsp cumin seeds
- 1 large onion, diced
- 1 tsp ginger and garlic paste
- ½ tsp turmeric
- 2 tomatoes, diced
- 6 cups spinach or a mixture of vegetables (mustard, kale, etc.)
- 2 tsp coriander powder
- 1 tsp cumin powder
- 2 tablespoon ground kasoori methi
- ½ tsp garam masala powder
- ¼ cup cream
- salt and pepper to taste

DIRECTIONS

1. Heat 2 tablespoon ghee in a heavy-bottomed pan. Brown the lamb cubes and place them in a pressure cooker. Cook up to 6-8 whistles. Remove from heat and set aside for steam to escape.
2. In the same pan used to brown the meat, add the red peppers, cinnamon, cardamom, and cloves.
3. Add the coriander seeds and cumin seeds. As soon as they start to crack, add the onions.
4. Fry the onions until it's almost golden.
5. Add ginger and garlic paste and turmeric. Cook until the rough odor disappears.
6. Cover and simmer until the tomatoes are tender. Add the vegetables. Thoroughly mix the vegetables and simmer for 5 min
7. Transfer to a blender. Mix until smooth.
8. Heat the remaining ghee in the earlier pan and add the mixed vegetable mixture. Add the coriander, cumin, and methi kasuri.
9. Cover and simmer for ten min Adjust the salt if necessary.
10. Cover and simmer the lamb for another 20 min, stirring frequently. Add water if necessary.
11. Add the cream and garam masala. Serve hot

NUTRITION

- Calories: 926
- Protein: 72.1 g
- Fat: 58.74 g
- Carbohydrates: 33 g

PREPARATION: 20 MIN **COOKING: 1H 20 MIN** **SERVES: 4**

71. ROGAN JOSH

INGREDIENTS

- 2 lbs. lamb shoulder cut into 1 to 2-inch pieces
- 2 tablespoon avocado oil or macadamia nut oil

Garlic and onion pasta:
- medium onion
- 8 garlic cloves

Spice blend:
- Bay leaves
- 10 whole cardamom pods
- 1 cinnamon stick
- ½ tsp ground cloves
- 1 tsp coriander
- 1 tsp cumin
- 2 tablespoon bell pepper
- 1 tsp cayenne pepper (reduce to ½ tsp if it is sensitive to spicy dishes. This dish is not so tasty, but in my opinion, it is a way)
- ¾ tsp salt
- 1 tsp pepper

Basic sauce:
- 3 relatively good medium-sized, russet, and chopped fresh tomatoes, but leave them a little thick. (remember the tomatoes are breaking up there, so don't make them too small)
- ¼ cup coconut milk or yogurt

DIRECTIONS

1. Put all the ingredients under the spice mix in a small bowl and keep cardamom, cinnamon, and bay leaves whole.
2. Blanch your fresh Roma tomatoes by soaking them in boiling water for about a minute or until they burst and let them cool, peel them, cut them, and reserve them.
3. Add garlic and onion to a mixer and mix until a relatively fine paste is obtained and place in a small bowl on the side.
4. Now that everything is ready to heat the oil in an oven over medium heat (or in a large pan)
5. Add the meat in batches if necessary and brown well on all sides.
6. Once all the meat is brown, put it back in the Dutch oven, lower the heat and add the onion and garlic paste with the spice mixture.
7. Mix thoroughly and make sure not to crush the bay leaves. Stir for 3 to 5 min or until very aromatic.
8. Add the chopped and blanched Roma tomatoes and coconut milk and stir until smooth.
9. Once it has been combined and boiled again on low heat, lower the temperature and place the lid on the Dutch oven and simmer for 1 hour and 15 min
10. Once cooked, serve with chopped fresh cilantro sprinkled on top.

NUTRITION

- Calories: 865
- Protein: 60.23 g
- Fat: 64.07 g
- Carbohydrates: 9.88 g

PREPARATION: 4 MIN

COOKING: 12 MIN

SERVES: 4

72. TILAPIA WITH PARMESAN BARK

INGREDIENTS

- ¾ cup freshly grated Parmesan cheese
- 2 teaspoons pepper
- 1 tablespoon chopped parsley
- 4 tilapia fillets (4 us)
- Lemon cut into pieces

DIRECTIONS

1. Set the oven to 400° F. Mix cheese in a shallow dish with pepper and parsley and season with salt and pepper.
2. Mix the fish in the cheese with olive oil and flirt. Place on a baking sheet with foil and bake for 10 to 12 minutes until the fish in the thickest part is opaque.
3. Serve the lemon slices with the fish.

NUTRITION

- Calories: 210
- Fat: 9.3g
- Net Carbs: 1.3g
- Protein: 28.9g

 **PREPARATION: 14 MIN**  **COOKING: 6 MIN**   **SERVES: 4**

73. BLACKENED FISH TACOS WITH SLAW

INGREDIENTS

- 1 tablespoon olive oil
- 1 teaspoon chili powder
- 2 tilapia fillets
- 1 teaspoon paprika
- 4 low carb tortillas

Slaw:
- ½ cup red cabbage, shredded
- 1 tablespoon lemon juice
- 1 teaspoon apple cider vinegar
- 1 tablespoon olive oil
- Salt and black pepper to taste

DIRECTIONS

1. Season the tilapia with chili powder and paprika. Heat the vegetable oil during a skillet over medium heat.
2. Add tilapia and cook until blackened, about 3 minutes per side. Cut into strips. Divide the tilapia between the tortillas. Blend all the slaw ingredients in a bowl and top the fish to serve.

NUTRITION

- Calories: 268
- Fat: 20g
- Net Carbs: 3.5g
- Protein: 13.8g

 **PREPARATION: 5 MIN**  **COOKING: 15 MIN**  **SERVES: 8**

74. MOZZARELLA FISH

INGREDIENTS

- 2 lbs. bone gold sole
- Salt and pepper to taste
- ½ teaspoon dried oregano
- 1 cup grated mozzarella cheese
- 1 large fresh tomato, sliced thinly

DIRECTIONS

1. Excellent source of cooking the butter. Organize a single layer of trout. Add salt, pepper, and oregano.
2. Top with sliced cheese slices and tomatoes.
3. Cook, covered, for 10 to 15 minutes at 425°F.

NUTRITION

- Calories: 156
- Fat: 6g
- Net Carbs: 5g
- Protein: 8g

PREPARATION: 10 MIN

COOKING: 30 MIN

SERVES: 5

75. CRAB CASSEROLE

INGREDIENTS

- 2 tablespoon oil, for frying
- 1 onion, finely chopped
- 150 g finely chopped celery stalks
- salt and pepper
- 300 ml homemade mayonnaise
- 4 eggs
- 450 g canned crab meat
- 325 g grated white cheddar cheese
- 2 teaspoon paprika
- ¼ teaspoon cayenne pepper

For filing
- 75 g leafy greens
- 2 tablespoon olive oil

DIRECTIONS

1. Set the oven to 350°F. Grease a 9x12 baking dish.
2. Fry onion and celery in oil until translucent.
3. In another bowl, add mayonnaise, eggs, crab meat, seasonings, and 2/3 chopped cheese. Add the fried onions and celery and stir.
4. Add the mass to the baking dish. Sprinkle the remaining cheese on top and bake for about 30 minutes or until golden brown.
5. Serve with salad and olive oil.

NUTRITION

- Carbohydrates: 6 g
- Fats: 95 g
- Proteins: 47 g
- Calories: 400

PREPARATION: 10 MIN **COOKING: 15 MIN** **SERVES: 4**

76. SALMON SKEWERS IN CURED HAM

INGREDIENTS

- Salmon Skewers
- 60 ml finely chopped fresh basil
- 450 g salmon
- salt black pepper
- 100 g dried ham sliced
- 1 tablespoon Olive oil
- 8 pcs wooden skewers
- 225 ml mayonnaise

DIRECTIONS

1. Soak the skewers in water.
2. Finely chop fresh basil.
3. Cut salmon fillet into rectangular pieces and fasten-on skewers.
4. Roll each kebab in the basil and pepper.
5. Cut the cured ham into thin slices and wrap her every kebab.
6. Lubricate with olive oil and fry in a pan, grill, or in the oven.
7. Serve with mayonnaise or salad

NUTRITION

- Carbohydrates: 1 g
- Fats: 62 g
- Proteins: 28 g
- Calories: 680

PREPARATION: 10 MIN

COOKING: 35 MIN

SERVES: 4

77. FISH CASSEROLE WITH CREAM CHEESE SAUCE

INGREDIENTS

- 280 g broccoli
- 280 g cooked fish
- 85 g grated Gouda cheese
- 1 teaspoon chopped green onions
- 1 liter water
- For the sauce:
- 119 ml fat cream
- 2 tablespoon grated Parmesan cheese
- 1 tablespoon butter
- 56.7 g cream cheese
- 1/4 teaspoon chopped garlic
- 1/8 teaspoon Chile
- Sea salt and black pepper to taste

DIRECTIONS

1. Preheat the oven to 350°F.
2. Set all the sauce ingredients into a saucepan and simmer for 3 minutes, stirring occasionally.
3. In another saucepan, bring the water to a boil and cook the broccoli for 3 minutes or until tender.
4. Mash the fish with a fork.
5. Put the broccoli in a casserole dish, put the chopped fish on top, pour the sauce and sprinkle with grated cheese.
6. Bake for at least 20 minutes or until golden brown.
7. Let stand for 5 minutes, sprinkle with chopped green onions and enjoy!

NUTRITION

- Carbohydrates: 9 g
- Fats: 36 g
- Proteins: 32 g

- Calories: 474

PREPARATION: 10 MIN | **COOKING: 20 MIN** | **SERVES: 2**

78. BACON AND JALAPENO WRAPPED SHRIMP

INGREDIENTS

- 4 jalapeño peppers, seedless and cut into 3 to 4 long strips each
- 12 large shrimp, deveined, butterflied, tail-on
- Salt
- Freshly ground black pepper
- 6 thin bacon slices
- ¼ cup shredded pepper jack cheese

DIRECTIONS

1. Preheat the oven to 350°F.
2. On a baking sheet, arrange the jalapeño strips in a single layer and roast for 10 minutes.
3. In a small bowl, season the shrimp with salt and pepper.
4. Remove the jalapeño strips from the oven. Place a strip inside each open butterflied shrimp. Wrap each shrimp with bacon and insert it with a toothpick. Organize in a single layer on a baking sheet.
5. Cook for 8 minutes until the bacon is crispy.
6. Adjust the oven to broil.
7. Sprinkle the cheese on top of the shrimp and broil for about 1 minute, until the cheese is bubbling.

NUTRITION

- Calories: 240
- Total Fat: 16 g
- Protein: 21 g
- Total Carbs: 3g
- Fiber: 1g
- Net Carbs: 2g

 **PREPARATION: 10 MIN**
 **COOKING: 10 MIN**
 **SERVES: 4**

79. CRISPY FISH STICK

INGREDIENTS

- 1 cup avocado oil or other cooking oil, plus more as needed
- 1-pound frozen cod, thawed
- 2 large eggs
- 2 tablespoons avocado oil mayonnaise
- 1 cup almond flour
- ½ cup grated Parmesan cheese
- ½ cup ground pork rinds
- ½ teaspoon chili powder
- ½ teaspoon chopped fresh parsley
- Salt
- Freshly ground black pepper
- ¼ cup Dairy-Free Tartar Sauce

DIRECTIONS

1. In a skillet, heat the avocado oil at high heat. You want the oil to be about ½ inch deep, so adjust the amount of oil-based on your pan's size.
2. Pat the dry fish using paper towels to remove any excess water.
3. In a small bowl, put the eggs and mayonnaise then whisk.
4. In another bowl, put the almond flour, Parmesan, pork rinds, chili powder, and parsley and mix well. Season with salt and pepper.
5. Cut the cod into strips.
6. Put the fish into the egg mixture then dredge in the dry mixture. Press the strips into the dry mixture so that the "breading" sticks well on all sides.
7. Add 3 to 4 fish sticks at a time to the hot oil. The oil should sizzle when you put the fish sticks. Cook for at least 2 minutes on each side, or until golden and crispy.
8. Place the cooked fish sticks on a paper towel-lined plate while you continue to fry the rest of the fish sticks.
9. Serve with the tartar sauce.

NUTRITION

- Calories: 402
- Total Fat: 30g
- Protein: 30g
- Total Carbs: 3g
- Fiber: 1g
- Net Carbs: 2g

PREPARATION: 5 MIN **COOKING: 10 MIN** **SERVES: 2**

80. PROSCIUTTO-WRAPPED COD

INGREDIENTS

- 2 (6-ounce) cod fillets
- Freshly ground black pepper
- 4 prosciutto slices
- 2 tablespoons butter or ghee

DIRECTIONS

1. Pat the dry fish using paper towels to remove any excess water.
2. Season the fillets with pepper and wrap the prosciutto around the fillets.
3. Heat a skillet at medium heat then add the butter.
4. Once the pan is hot, add the fillets and cook on each side for 5 minutes, up to the outside is crispy and the inside is flaky.
5. Place the cooked fish onto a paper towel-lined plate to absorb any excess oil.

NUTRITION

- Calories: 317
- Total Fat: 18g
- Protein: 38g
- Total Carbs: 0g
- Fiber: 0g
- Net Carbs: 0g

PREPARATION: 10 MIN COOKING: 10 MIN SERVES: 2

81. COCONUT MAHI-MAHI NUGGETS

INGREDIENTS

- 1 cup avocado oil or coconut oil, plus more as needed
- 1-pound frozen mahi-mahi, thawed
- 2 large eggs
- 2 tablespoons avocado oil mayonnaise
- 1 cup almond flour
- ½ cup shredded coconut
- ¼ cup crushed macadamia nuts
- Salt
- Freshly ground black pepper
- ½ lime, cut into wedges
- ¼ cup Dairy-Free Tartar Sauce

DIRECTIONS

1. In a skillet, warm the avocado oil at high heat. You want the oil to be about ½ inch deep, so adjust the amount of oil-based on the size of your pan.
2. Pat the fish to try using paper towels to take off any excess water.
3. In a small bowl, put and combine the eggs and mayonnaise.
4. In a medium mixing bowl, put and combine the almond flour, coconut, and macadamia nuts. Season with salt and pepper. Cut the mahi-mahi into nuggets.
5. Put the fish into the egg mixture then dredge in the dry mix. Press into the dry mixture so that "breading" sticks well on all sides.
6. Add the fish to the hot oil. It should sizzle when you add the nuggets. Cook for 2 minutes per side, until golden and crispy.
7. Place the cooked nuggets on a paper towel-lined plate and squirt the lime wedges over them.

NUTRITION

- Calories: 733
- Total Fat: 53g
- Protein: 54g
- Total Carbs: 10g
- Fiber: 6g
- Net Carbs: 4g

PREPARATION: 10 MIN

COOKING: 10 MIN

SERVES: 6

82. GARLIC & GINGER CHICKEN WITH PEANUT SAUCE

INGREDIENTS

Chicken ingredients
- 1 tbsp wheat-free soy sauce
- 1 tbsp sugar-free fish sauce
- 1 tbsp lime juice
- 1 tsp cilantro, chopped
- 1 minced garlic
- 1 tsp minced ginger
- 1 tbsp olive oil
- 1 tbsp rice wine vinegar
- 1 tsp cayenne pepper
- 1 tbsp erythritol
- 6 chicken thighs

Peanut sauce
- ½ cup peanut butter
- 1 tsp minced garlic
- 1 tbsp lime juice
- 2 tbsp water
- 1 tsp minced ginger
- 1 tbsp jalapeño pepper, chopped
- 2 tbsp rice wine vinegar
- 2 tbsp erythritol
- 1 tbsp fish sauce

DIRECTIONS

1. Combine all chicken ingredients in a large Ziploc bag. Seal the bag and shake to combine. Refrigerate for 1 hour. Remove from the fridge about 15 minutes before cooking. Preheat the grill to medium heat.
2. Cook the chicken for 7 minutes per side until golden brown. Remove to a serving plate. Whisk together all the sauce ingredients in a mixing bowl. Serve the chicken drizzled with peanut sauce.

NUTRITION

- Calories: 492
- Fat: 36g
- Net Carbs: 3g
- Protein: 35g

PREPARATION: 10 MIN

COOKING: 20 MIN

SERVES: 4

83. EASY CHICKEN CHILI

INGREDIENTS

- 4 chicken breasts
- 2 tbsp butter
- 1 onion, chopped
- 8 oz diced tomatoes
- 2 tbsp tomato puree
- ½ tsp chili powder
- ½ tsp cumin
- ½ tsp garlic powder
- 1 serrano pepper, minced
- ½ cup cheddar cheese, shredded
- Salt and black pepper to taste

DIRECTIONS

1. Put a large saucepan over medium heat and add the chicken. Cover with water and bring to a boil. Cook for 10 minutes. Transfer the chicken to a flat surface and shred with forks. Reserve 2 cups of the broth.
2. Melt the butter in a large pot over medium heat. Sauté onion until transparent for 3 minutes. Stir in the chicken, tomatoes, cumin, serrano pepper, garlic powder, tomato puree, broth, and chili powder. Adjust the seasoning and let the mixture boil. Simmer for 10 minutes. Top with shredded cheese and serve.

NUTRITION

- Calories: 421
- Fat: 21g
- Net Carbs: 5.6g
- Protein: 45g

PREPARATION: 15 MIN

COOKING: 30 MIN

SERVES: 4

84. EGGPLANT & TOMATO BRAISED CHICKEN THIGHS

INGREDIENTS

- 2 tbsp ghee
- 1 lb. chicken thighs
- Salt and black pepper to taste
- 2 garlic cloves, minced
- 1 (14 oz) can whole tomatoes
- 1 eggplant, diced

DIRECTIONS

1. Melt ghee in a saucepan over medium heat. Season the chicken with salt and black pepper and fry for 4 minutes on each side until golden brown. Remove to a plate. Sauté the garlic in the ghee for 2 minutes.
2. Pour in the tomatoes and cook covered for 8 minutes. Add in the eggplant and sauté for 4 minutes. Adjust the seasoning with salt and black pepper. Stir and add the chicken. Coat with sauce and simmer for 3 minutes. Serve chicken with sauce on a bed of squash pasta.

NUTRITION

- Calories: 468
- Fat: 39.5g
- Net Carbs: 2g,
- Protein: 26g

PREPARATION: 10 MIN

COOKING: 10 MIN

SERVES: 4

85. LEMON-GARLIC CHICKEN SKEWERS

INGREDIENTS

- 1 lb. chicken breasts, cut into cubes
- 2 tbsp olive oil
- 2/3 jar preserved lemon, drained
- 2 garlic cloves, minced
- ½ cup lemon juice
- Salt and black pepper to taste
- 1 tsp fresh rosemary, chopped
- 4 lemon wedges

DIRECTIONS

1. In a wide bowl, mix half of the oil, garlic, salt, pepper, and lemon juice and add the chicken cubes and lemon rind. Let marinate for 2 hours in the refrigerator. Remove the chicken and thread it onto skewers.
2. Heat a grill pan over high heat. Add in the chicken skewers and sear them for 6 minutes per side. Remove to a plate and serve warm garnished with rosemary and lemons wedges.

NUTRITION

- Calories: 350
- Fat: 11g
- Net Carbs: 3.5g
- Protein: 34g

 **PREPARATION: 5 MIN**

 **COOKING: 25 MIN**

 **SERVES: 6**

86. SWEET CHILI GRILLED CHICKEN

INGREDIENTS

- 2 lb. chicken breasts
- 4 cloves garlic, minced
- 2 tbsp fresh oregano, chopped
- ½ cup lemon juice
- 2/3 cup olive oil
- 1 tbsp erythritol
- Salt and black pepper to taste
- 3 small chilies, minced

DIRECTIONS

1. Preheat grill to high heat. In a bowl, mix the garlic, oregano, lemon juice, olive oil, chilies, and erythritol. Cover the chicken with plastic wraps and use the rolling pin to pound to ½-inch thickness.
2. Remove the wrap and brush the spice mixture on the chicken on all sides. Place on the grill and cook for 15 minutes, flip, and continue cooking for 10 more minutes. Remove to a plate and serve with salad.

NUTRITION

- Calories: 265
- Fat: 9g
- Net Carbs: 3g
- Protein: 26g

PREPARATION: 5 MIN

COOKING: 45 MIN

SERVES: 4

87. CHICKEN & SQUASH TRAYBAKE

INGREDIENTS

- 1 ½ lb. chicken thighs
- 1 lb. butternut squash, cubed
- ½ cup black olives, pitted
- ¼ cup olive oil
- 5 garlic cloves, sliced
- ¼ tbsp dried oregano

DIRECTIONS

1. Preheat oven to 400°F. Place the chicken in a greased baking dish with the skin down. Place the garlic, olives, and butternut squash around the chicken. Drizzle with olive oil. Sprinkle with black pepper, salt, and oregano.
2. Bake in the oven for 45 minutes until golden brown. Serve warm.

NUTRITION

- Calories: 411
- Fat: 15g
- Net Carbs: 5.5g
- Protein: 31g

9. VEGETABLES RECIPES

PREPARATION: 7 MIN

COOKING: 15 MIN

SERVES: 2

88. FRIED GARLIC BACON AND BOK CHOY BROTH

INGREDIENTS

- 2 cups bok choy, chopped
- A drizzle avocado oil
- 2 bacon slices, chopped
- 2 garlic cloves, minced
- Black pepper
- Salt

DIRECTIONS

1. Put bacon in a pan on medium heat and let crisp. Remove and let drain on paper towels.
2. Add bok choy and garlic to the pan and let cook for 4 minutes.
3. Season with pepper and salt and put the bacon back into the pan.
4. Let cook for 1 minute and serve.

NUTRITION

- Calories: 116
- Carbs: 8g
- Protein: 3g
- Fiber: 8g
- Fats: 1g

PREPARATION: 5 MIN

COOKING: 10 MIN

SERVES: 2

89. JICAMA FRIES

INGREDIENTS

- 1 Jicama (sliced into thin strips)
- 1/2 teaspoon onion powder
- 2 tablespoons avocado oil
- Cayenne pepper (pinch)
- 1 teaspoon paprika
- Sea salt, to taste

DIRECTIONS

1. Dry roast the jicama strips in a non-stick frying pan (or you can also grease the pan with a bit of avocado oil)
2. Place the roasted jicama fries into a large bowl and add the onion powder, cayenne pepper, paprika, and sea salt.
3. Drizzle over the avocado oil and toss the contents until the flavors are incorporated well.
4. Serve immediately and enjoy!

NUTRITION

- Calories: 92
- Fat: 7 g
- Protein: 1 g
- Net Carb: 2 g

PREPARATION: 5 MIN **COOKING: 25 MIN** **SERVES: 4**

90. CURRY SPICED ALMONDS

INGREDIENTS

- 1 cup whole almonds
- 2 teaspoons olive oil
- 1 teaspoon curry powder
- ¼ teaspoon salt
- ¼ teaspoon ground turmeric
- Pinch cayenne

DIRECTIONS

1. Preheat the oven to 300°F
2. In a mixing bowl, whisk the spices and olive oil.
3. Toss in the almonds then spread on the baking sheet.
4. Bake for 25 minutes until toasted, then cool and store in an airtight container.

NUTRITION

- Calories: 155
- Fat: 14g
- Protein: 5g
- Net Carbs: 2g

 **PREPARATION: 10 MIN**    **COOKING: 12 MIN**    **SERVES: 2**

91. SALTED KALE CHIPS

INGREDIENTS

- ½ bunch fresh kale
- 1 tablespoon olive oil
- Salt and pepper to taste

DIRECTIONS

1. Preheat the oven to 350°F and line a baking sheet with foil.
2. Pick the thick stems from the kale and then tear the leaves into pieces.
3. Toss the kale with olive oil and spread it on the baking sheet.
4. Bake for 10 to 12 minutes until crisp, then sprinkle with salt and pepper.

NUTRITION

- Calories: 75
- Fat: 7g
- Protein: 1g
- Net Carbs: 3g

PREPARATION: 5 MIN **COOKING: 5 MIN** **SERVES: 2**

92. TOASTED PUMPKIN SEEDS

INGREDIENTS

- ½ cup hulled pumpkin seeds
- 2 teaspoons coconut oil
- 2 teaspoons chili powder
- ½ teaspoon salt

DIRECTIONS

1. Heat a cast-iron skillet over medium heat.
2. Add the pumpkin seeds and let them cook until toasted, about 3 to 5 minutes, stirring often.
3. Remove from heat and stir in the coconut oil, chili powder, and salt.
4. Let the seeds cool, then store them in an airtight container.

NUTRITION

- Calories: 100
- Fat: 8.5g
- Protein: 5.5g
- Net Carbs: 0.5g

PREPARATION: 5 MIN

COOKING: 15 MIN

SERVES: 6

93. CAULIFLOWER CHEESE DIP

INGREDIENTS

- One small head cauliflower, chopped
- ¾ cup chicken broth
- ¼ teaspoon ground cumin
- ¼ teaspoon chili powder
- ¼ teaspoon garlic powder
- Salt and pepper to taste
- 1/3 cup cream cheese, chopped
- Two tablespoons canned coconut milk

DIRECTIONS

1. Combine the cauliflower and chicken broth in a saucepan and simmer until the cauliflower is tender.
2. Add the cumin, chili powder, and garlic powder, then season with salt and pepper.
3. Stir in the cream cheese until melted, then blend everything with an immersion blender.
4. Whisk in the coconut milk, then spoon into a serving bowl.
5. Serve with sliced celery sticks.

NUTRITION

- Calories: 75
- Fat: 6g
- Protein: 2.5g
- Net Carbs: 2g

PREPARATION: 10 MIN

COOKING: 3 HOURS

SERVES: 4

94. BUTTER GREEN PEAS

INGREDIENTS

- 1 cup green peas
- 1 teaspoon minced garlic
- 1 tablespoon butter, softened
- ½ teaspoon cayenne pepper
- 1 tablespoon olive oil
- ¾ teaspoon salt
- 1 teaspoon paprika
- 1 teaspoon garam masala
- ½ cup chicken stock

DIRECTIONS

1. In the slow cooker, mix the peas with butter, garlic, and the other ingredients,
2. Close the lid then cook it for 3 hours on High.

NUTRITION

- Calories: 121
- Fat: 6.5g
- Fiber: 3
- Carbs: 3.4
- Protein: 0.6

PREPARATION: 8 MIN

COOKING: 5 HOURS

SERVES: 2

95. LEMON ASPARAGUS

INGREDIENTS

- 8 oz asparagus
- ½ cup butter
- Juice of 1 lemon
- Zest of 1 lemon, grated
- ½ teaspoon turmeric
- 1 teaspoon rosemary, dried

DIRECTIONS

1. In your slow cooker, mix the asparagus with butter, lemon juice, and the other ingredients and close the lid.
2. Cook the vegetables on Low for 5 hours. Divide between plates and serve.

NUTRITION

- Calories: 139
- Fat: 4.6g
- Fiber: 2.5g
- Carbs: 3.3g
- Protein: 3.5g

PREPARATION: 10 MIN   **COOKING: 2H 30 MIN**   **SERVES: 5**

96. LIME GREEN BEANS

INGREDIENTS

- 1-pound green beans, trimmed and halved
- 2 spring onions, chopped
- 2 tablespoons lime juice
- ½ teaspoon lime zest, grated
- 2 tablespoons olive oil
- ¼ teaspoon ground black pepper
- ¾ teaspoon salt
- ¾ cup water

DIRECTIONS

1. In the slow cooker, mix the green beans with the spring onions and the other ingredients and close the lid.
2. Cook for 2.5 hours on High.

NUTRITION

- Calories: 67
- Fat: 5.6g
- Fiber: 2g
- Carbs: 4g
- Protein: 2.1g

 **PREPARATION: 10 MIN**  **COOKING: 3 HOURS**  **SERVES: 4**

97. CHEESE ASPARAGUS

INGREDIENTS

- 10 oz asparagus, trimmed
- 4 oz Cheddar cheese, sliced
- 1/3 cup butter, soft
- 1 teaspoon turmeric powder
- ½ teaspoon salt
- ¼ teaspoon white pepper

DIRECTIONS

1. In the slow cooker, mix the asparagus with butter and the other ingredients, put the lid on, and cook for 3 hours on High.

NUTRITION

- Calories: 214
- Fat: 6.2g
- Fiber: 1.7g
- Carbs: 3.6g
- Protein: 4.2g

PREPARATION: 15 MIN **COOKING: 1 HOUR** **SERVES: 4**

98. CREAMY BROCCOLI

INGREDIENTS

- ½ cup coconut cream
- 2 cups broccoli florets
- 1 teaspoon mint, dried
- 1 teaspoon garam masala
- 1 teaspoon salt
- 1 tablespoon almonds flakes
- ½ teaspoon turmeric

DIRECTIONS

1. In the slow cooker, mix the broccoli with the mint and the other ingredients.
2. Close the lid and cook vegetables for 1 hour on High.
3. Divide between plates and serve.

NUTRITION

- Calories: 102
- Fat: 9g
- Fiber: 1.9g
- Carbs: 4.3g
- Protein: 2.5g

PREPARATION: 15 MIN

COOKING: 2 HOURS

SERVES: 4

99. GARLIC EGGPLANT

INGREDIENTS

- 1-pound eggplant, trimmed and roughly cubed
- 1 tablespoon balsamic vinegar
- 1 garlic clove, diced
- 1 teaspoon tarragon
- 1 teaspoon salt
- 1 tablespoon olive oil
- ½ teaspoon ground paprika
- ¼ cup water

DIRECTIONS

1. In the slow cooker, mix the eggplant with the vinegar, garlic, and the other ingredients, close the lid and cook on High for 2 hours.
2. Divide into bowls and serve.

NUTRITION

- Calories: 132
- Fat: 2.8g
- Fiber: 4.7g
- Carbs: 8.5g
- Protein: 1.6g

PREPARATION: 10 MIN

COOKING: 4 HOURS

SERVES: 6

100. COCONUT BRUSSELS SPROUTS

INGREDIENTS

- 2 cups Brussels sprouts, halved
- ½ cup coconut milk
- 1 teaspoon garlic powder
- 1 teaspoon salt
- ½ teaspoon coriander, ground
- 1 teaspoon dried oregano
- 1 tablespoon balsamic vinegar
- 1 teaspoon butter

DIRECTIONS

1. Place Brussels sprouts in the slow cooker.
2. Add the rest of the ingredients, toss, close the lid and cook the Brussels sprouts for 4 hours on Low.
3. Divide between plates and serve.

NUTRITION

- Calories: 128
- Fat: 5.6g
- Fiber: 1.7g
- Carbs: 4.4g
- Protein: 3.6g2

 **PREPARATION: 15 MIN**  **COOKING: 2 HOURS**   **SERVES: 6**

101. CAULIFLOWER PILAF WITH HAZELNUTS

INGREDIENTS

- 3 cups cauliflower, chopped
- 1 cup chicken stock
- 1 teaspoon ground black pepper
- ½ teaspoon turmeric
- ½ teaspoon ground paprika
- 1 teaspoon salt
- 1 tablespoon dried dill
- 1 tablespoon butter
- 2 tablespoons hazelnuts, chopped

DIRECTIONS

1. Put cauliflower in the blender and blend until you get cauliflower rice.
2. Then transfer the cauliflower rice to the slow cooker.
3. Add ground black pepper, turmeric, ground paprika, salt, dried dill, and butter.
4. Mix up the cauliflower rice. Add chicken stock and close the lid.
5. Cook the pilaf for 2 hours on High.
6. Then add chopped hazelnuts and mix u the pilaf well.

NUTRITION

- Calories: 48
- Fat: 3.1g
- Fiber: 1.9g
- Carbs: 4.8g
- Protein: 1.6g

PREPARATION: 10 MIN **COOKING: 3 HOURS** **SERVES: 3**

102. CAULIFLOWER AND TURMERIC MASH

INGREDIENTS

- 1 cup cauliflower florets
- 1 teaspoon turmeric powder
- 1 cup water
- 1 teaspoon salt
- 1 tablespoon butter
- 1 tablespoon coconut cream
- 1 teaspoon coriander, ground

DIRECTIONS

1. In the slow cooker, mix the cauliflower with water and salt.
2. Close the lid then cook it for 3 hours on High.
3. Then drain water and transfer the cauliflower to a blender.
4. Add the rest of the ingredients, blend and serve.

NUTRITION

- Calories: 58
- Fat: 5.2g
- Fiber: 1.2g
- Carbs: 2.7g
- Protein: 1.1g

PREPARATION: 15 MIN

COOKING: 3H 30 MIN

SERVES: 6

103. SPINACH AND OLIVES MIX

INGREDIENTS

- 2 cups spinach
- 2 tablespoons chives, chopped
- 5 oz Cheddar cheese, shredded
- ½ cup heavy cream
- 1 teaspoon ground black pepper
- ½ teaspoon salt
- 1 cup black olives, pitted and halved
- 1 teaspoon sage
- 1 teaspoon sweet paprika

DIRECTIONS

1. In the slow cooker, mix the spinach with the chives and the other ingredients, toss and close the lid.
2. Cook for 3.5 hours on Low and serve.

NUTRITION

- Calories: 189
- Fat: 6.2g
- Fiber: 0.6g
- Carbs: 3g
- Protein: 3.4g

PREPARATION: 15 MIN

COOKING: 6 HOURS

SERVES: 4

104. RED CABBAGE AND WALNUTS

INGREDIENTS

- 2 cups red cabbage, shredded
- 3 spring onions, chopped
- ½ cup chicken stock
- 1 tablespoon olive oil
- 1 teaspoon salt
- 1 teaspoon cumin, ground
- 1 teaspoon hot paprika
- 1 tablespoon keto tomato sauce
- 1 oz walnuts
- 1/3 cup fresh parsley, chopped

DIRECTIONS

1. In the slow cooker, mix the cabbage with the spring onions and the other ingredients.
2. Close the lid and cook cabbage for 6 hours on Low.
3. Divide into bowls and serve.

NUTRITION

- Calories: 112
- Fat: 5.1g
- Fiber: 2g
- Carbs: 5.8g
- Protein: 3.5g

PREPARATION: 15 MIN | **COOKING: 2H 30 MIN** | **SERVES: 6**

105. PAPRIKA BOK CHOY

INGREDIENTS

- 1-pound bok choy, torn
- ½ cup coconut milk
- 1 tablespoon almond butter, softened
- 1 teaspoon ground paprika
- 1 teaspoon turmeric
- ½ teaspoon cayenne pepper

DIRECTIONS

1. In the slow cooker, mix the bok choy with the coconut milk and the other ingredients, toss and close the lid.
2. Cook the meal for 2.5 hours on High.

NUTRITION

- Calories: 128
- Fat: 3.2g
- Fiber: 3.9g
- Carbs: 4.9g
- Protein: 4.1g

PREPARATION: 10 MIN   **COOKING: 3 HOURS**   **SERVES: 6**

106. ZUCCHINI MIX

INGREDIENTS

- 1-pound zucchinis, roughly cubed
- 2 spring onions, chopped
- 1 teaspoon curry paste
- 1 teaspoon basil, dried
- 1 teaspoon salt
- 1 teaspoon ground black pepper
- 1 bay leaf
- ½ cup beef stock

DIRECTIONS

1. In the slow cooker, mix the zucchinis with the onion and the other ingredients.
2. Close the lid then cook it on Low for 3 hours.

NUTRITION

- Calories: 34
- Fat: 1.3g
- Fiber: 3.6g
- Carbs: 4.7g
- Protein: 3.6g

 **PREPARATION: 20 MIN**    **COOKING: 2 HOURS**    **SERVES: 8**

107. ZUCCHINI AND SPRING ONIONS

INGREDIENTS

- 1-pound zucchinis, sliced
- 1 teaspoon avocado oil
- 1 teaspoon salt
- 1 teaspoon white pepper
- 2 spring onions, chopped
- 1/3 cup organic almond milk
- 2 tablespoons butter
- ½ teaspoon turmeric powder

DIRECTIONS

1. In the slow cooker, mix the zucchinis with the spring onions, oil, and the other ingredients.
2. Close the lid then cook it for 2 hours on High.

NUTRITION

- Calories: 82
- Fat: 5.6g
- Fiber: 2.8g
- Carbs: 5.6g
- Protein: 3.2g

PREPARATION: 15 MIN

COOKING: 7 HOURS

SERVES: 4

108. CREAMY PORTOBELLO MIX

INGREDIENTS

- 4 Portobello mushrooms
- ½ cup Monterey Jack cheese, grated
- ½ cup heavy cream
- 1 teaspoon curry powder
- 1 teaspoon basil, dried
- ½ teaspoon salt
- 1 teaspoon olive oil

DIRECTIONS

1. In the slow cooker, mix the mushrooms with the cheese and the other ingredients.
2. Close the lid and cook the meal for 7 hours on Low.

NUTRITION

- Calories: 126
- Fat: 5.1g
- Fiber: 1.6g
- Carbs: 5.9g
- Protein: 4.4g

 **PREPARATION: 10 MIN**

 **COOKING: 2H 30 MIN**

 SERVES: 2

109. EGGPLANT MASH

INGREDIENTS

- 7 oz eggplant, trimmed
- 1 tablespoon butter
- 1 teaspoon basil, dried
- 1 teaspoon chili powder
- ½ teaspoon garlic powder
- 1/3 cup water
- ½ teaspoon salt

DIRECTIONS

1. Peel the eggplant and rub it with salt.
2. Then put it in the slow cooker plus add the water.
3. Close the lid and cook the eggplant for 2.5 hours on High.
4. Then drain water and mash the eggplant.
5. Add the rest of the ingredients, whisk and serve.

NUTRITION

- Calories: 206
- Fat: 6.2g
- Fiber: 3.6g
- Carbs: 7.9g
- Protein: 8.6g

PREPARATION: 15 MIN

COOKING: 3 HOURS

SERVES: 6

110. CHEDDAR ARTICHOKE

INGREDIENTS

- 1 teaspoon garlic, diced
- 1 tablespoon olive oil
- 1-pound artichoke hearts, chopped
- 3 oz Cheddar cheese, shredded
- 1 teaspoon curry powder
- 1 cup chicken stock
- 1 teaspoon butter
- 1 teaspoon garam masala

DIRECTIONS

1. In the slow cooker, mix the artichokes with garlic, oil, and other ingredients.
2. Cook the artichoke hearts for 3 hours on High.
3. Divide between plates and serve.

NUTRITION

- Calories: 135
- Fat: 3.9g
- Fiber: 4.3g
- Carbs: 4.9g
- Protein: 4.3g

PREPARATION: 15 MIN

COOKING: 4 HOURS

SERVES: 6

111. SQUASH AND ZUCCHINIS

INGREDIENTS

- 4 cups spaghetti squash, cubed
- 2 zucchinis, cubed
- ½ cup coconut milk
- ½ teaspoon ground cinnamon
- ¾ teaspoon ground ginger
- 3 tablespoons oregano
- 1 teaspoon butter

DIRECTIONS

1. In the slow cooker, mix the squash with the zucchinis, milk, and other ingredients.
2. Close the lid and cook the vegetables on Low for 4 hours.

NUTRITION

- Calories: 40
- Fat: 2.2g
- Fiber: 1.8g
- Carbs: 4.3g
- Protein: 1.1g

 **PREPARATION: 10 MIN**  **COOKING: 3 HOURS**  **SERVES: 3**

112. DILL LEEKS

INGREDIENTS

- 2 cups leeks, sliced
- 1 cup chicken stock
- 2 tablespoons fresh dill, chopped
- ½ teaspoon turmeric powder
- 1 teaspoon sweet paprika
- 1 tablespoon coconut cream
- 1 teaspoon butter

DIRECTIONS

1. In the slow cooker, mix the beets with the stock, dill, and other ingredients.
2. Cook on Low for 3 hours and serve.

NUTRITION

- Calories: 123
- Fat: 2.9g
- Fiber: 2.2g
- Carbs: 7.5g
- Protein: 4.3g

PREPARATION: 20 MIN **COOKING: 6 HOURS** **SERVES: 4**

113. VEGETABLE LASAGNA

INGREDIENTS

- 1 eggplant, sliced
- 1 cup kale, chopped
- 3 eggs, beaten
- 2 tablespoons keto tomato sauce
- ½ teaspoon ground black pepper
- 1 cup Cheddar, grated
- ½ teaspoon chili flakes
- 1 tablespoon tomato sauce
- 1 teaspoon coconut oil
- ½ teaspoon butter

DIRECTIONS

1. Place coconut oil in the skillet and melt it.
2. Then add sliced eggplants and roast them for 1 minute from each side.
3. After this, transfer them in the bowl.
4. Toss butter in the skillet.
5. Place 1 beaten egg in the skillet and stir it to get the shape of a pancake.
6. Roast the egg pancake for 1 minute from each side.
7. Repeat the steps with the remaining eggs.
8. Separate the eggplants into 2 parts.
9. Place 1 part of eggplants in the slow cooker. You should make the eggplant layer.
10. Then add ½ cup chopped parsley and 1 egg pancake.
11. Sprinkle the egg pancakes with 1/3 cup of Parmesan.
12. Then add remaining eggplants and second egg pancake.
13. Sprinkle it with ½ part of remaining Parmesan and top with the last egg pancake.
14. Then spread it with tomato sauce, kale and sprinkle with chili flakes and ground black pepper.
15. Add tomato sauce and top lasagna with remaining cheese.
16. Close the lid and cook lasagna for 6 hours on Low.

NUTRITION

- Calories: 257
- Fat: 15.9g
- Fiber: 4.5g
- Carbs: 10.5g
- Protein: 21.5g

10. POULTRY AND EGGS RECIPES

PREPARATION: 120 MIN	**COOKING: 40 MIN**	**SERVES: 8**

114. TASTY CHICKEN WITH BRUSSELS SPROUTS

INGREDIENTS

- 5 pounds whole chicken
- 1 bunch oregano
- 1 bunch thyme
- 1 tablespoon marjoram
- 1 tablespoon parsley
- 1 tablespoon olive oil
- 2 pounds Brussels sprouts
- 1 lemon
- 4 tablespoon butter

DIRECTIONS

1. Preheat your oven to 450°F.
2. Stuff the chicken with oregano, thyme, and lemon.
3. Make sure the wings are tucked over and behind.
4. Roast for 15 minutes. Reduce the heat to 325°F, and cook for 40 minutes.
5. Spread the butter over the chicken and sprinkle parsley and marjoram.
6. Add the Brussels sprouts. Return to oven and bake for 40 more minutes.
7. Let sit for 10 minutes before carving.

NUTRITION

- Calories: 430
- Net Carbs: 5g
- Fat: 32g
- Protein: 30g

PREPARATION: 5 MIN   **COOKING: 10 MIN**   **SERVES: 2**

115. CHAFFLES WITH SCRAMBLED EGGS

INGREDIENTS

- 2 teaspoon coconut flour
- ½ cup shredded cheddar cheese, full-fat
- 3 eggs
- 1-ounce butter, unsalted
- Seasoning:
- ¼ teaspoon salt
- 1/8 teaspoon ground black pepper
- 1/8 teaspoon dried oregano

DIRECTIONS

1. Switch on a mini waffle maker and let it preheat for 5 minutes.
2. Meanwhile, take a medium bowl, place all the ingredients in it, reserving 2 eggs and then mix by using an immersion blender until smooth.
3. Ladle the batter evenly into the waffle maker, shut with lid, and let it cook for 3 to 4 minutes until firm and golden brown.
4. Meanwhile, prepare scrambled eggs and for this, take a medium bowl, crack the eggs in it and whisk them with a fork until frothy, and then season with salt and black pepper.
5. Take a medium skillet pan, place it over medium heat, add butter and when it melts, pour in eggs and cook for 2 minutes until creamy, stirring continuously.
6. Top chaffles with scrambled eggs, sprinkle with oregano and then serve.

NUTRITION

- Calories: 265
- Fats: 18.5g
- Protein: 17.6g
- Net Carb: 3.4g
- Fiber: 6g

PREPARATION: 10 MIN **COOKING: 3 HOURS** **SERVES: 4**

116. AROMATIC JALAPENO WINGS

INGREDIENTS

- 1 jalapeño pepper, diced
- ½ cup fresh cilantro, diced
- 3 tablespoon coconut oil
- Juice from 1 lime
- 2 garlic cloves, peeled and minced
- Salt and black pepper ground, to taste
- 2 lbs. chicken wings
- Lime wedges, to serve
- Mayonnaise, to serve

DIRECTIONS

1. Start by throwing all the fixings into the large bowl and mix well.
2. Cover the wings and marinate them in the refrigerator for 2 hours.
3. Now add the wings along with their marinade into the Crockpot.
4. Cover it and cook for 3 hours on Low Settings.
5. Garnish as desired.
6. Serve warm.

NUTRITION

- Calories: 246
- Total Fat: 7.4 g
- Saturated Fat: 4.6 g
- Cholesterol: 105 mg
- Total Carbs: 9.4 g
- Sugar: 6.5 g
- Fiber: 2.7 g
- Sodium: 353 mg
- Potassium: 529 mg
- Protein: 37.2 g

 **PREPARATION: 10 MIN**

 **COOKING: 3 HOURS**

 **SERVES: 4**

117. BARBEQUE CHICKEN WINGS

INGREDIENTS

- 2 lbs. chicken wings
- 1/2 cup water
- 1/2 teaspoon of basil, dried
- 3/4 cup BBQ sauce
- 1/2 cup lime juice
- 1 teaspoon red pepper, crushed
- 2 teaspoons paprika
- 1/2 cup swerve
- Salt and black pepperto taste
- A pinch cayenne peppers

DIRECTIONS

1. Start by throwing all the fixings into the Crockpot and mix them well.
2. Cover it and cook for 3 hours on Low Settings.
3. Garnish as desired.
4. Serve warm.

NUTRITION

- Calories: 457
- Total Fat: 19.1 g
- Saturated Fat: 11 g
- Cholesterol: 262 mg
- Total Carbs: 8.9 g
- Sugar: 1.2 g
- Fiber: 1.7 g
- Sodium: 557 mg
- Potassium: 748 mg
- Protein: 32.5 g

PREPARATION: 10 MIN **COOKING: 6 HOURS** **SERVES: 4**

118. SAUCY DUCK

INGREDIENTS

- 1 duck, cut into small chunks
- 4 garlic cloves, minced
- 4 tablespoons swerves
- 2 green onions, roughly diced
- 4 tablespoon soy sauce
- 4 tablespoon sherry wine
- 1/4 cup water
- 1-inch ginger root, sliced
- A pinch salt
- black pepper to taste

DIRECTIONS

1. Start by throwing all the fixings into the Crockpot and mix them well.
2. Cover it and cook for 6 hours on Low Settings.
3. Garnish as desired.
4. Serve warm.

NUTRITION

- Calories: 338
- Total Fat: 3.8 g
- Saturated Fat: 0.7 g
- Cholesterol: 22 mg
- Total Carbs: 8.3 g
- Fiber: 2.4 g
- Sugar: 1.2 g
- Sodium: 620 mg
- Potassium: 271 mg
- Protein: 15.4g

PREPARATION: 10 MIN   **COOKING: 6 HOURS**   **SERVES: 24**

119. CHICKEN ROUX GUMBO

INGREDIENTS

- 1 lb. chicken thighs, cut into halves
- 1 tablespoon vegetable oil
- 1 lb. smoky sausage, sliced, crispy, and crumbled.
- Salt and black pepperto taste

Aromatics:
- 1 bell pepper, diced
- 2 quarts' chicken stock
- 15 oz. canned tomatoes, diced
- 1 celery stalk, diced
- salt to taste
- 4 garlic cloves, minced
- 1/2 lbs. okra, sliced
- 1 yellow onion, diced
- a dash tabasco sauce

For the roux:
- 1/2 cup almond flour
- 1/4 cup vegetable oil
- 1 teaspoon Cajun spice

DIRECTIONS

1. Start by throwing all the ingredients except okra and roux Ingredients: into the Crockpot.
2. Cover it and cook for 5 hours on Low Settings.
3. Stir in okra and cook for another 1 hour on low heat.
4. Mix all the roux Ingredients: and add them to the Crockpot.
5. Stir cook on high heat until the sauce thickens.
6. Garnish as desired.
7. Serve warm.

NUTRITION

- Calories: 604
- Total Fat: 30.6 g
- Saturated Fat: 13.1 g
- Cholesterol: 131 mg
- Total Carbs:1.4g
- Fiber: 0.2 g
- Sugar: 20.3 g
- Sodium: 834 mg
- Potassium: 512 mg
- Protein: 54.6 g

PREPARATION: 10 MIN   **COOKING: 5 HOURS**   **SERVES: 2**

120. CIDER-BRAISED CHICKEN

INGREDIENTS

- 4 chicken drumsticks
- 2 tablespoon olive oil
- ½ cup apple cider vinegar
- 1 tablespoon balsamic vinegar
- 1 chili pepper, diced
- 1 yellow onion, minced
- Salt and black pepper to taste

DIRECTIONS

1. Start by throwing all the ingredients into a bowl and mix them well.
2. Marinate this chicken for 2 hours in the refrigerator.
3. Spread the chicken along with its marinade in the Crockpot.
4. Cover it and cook for 5 hours on Low Settings.
5. Garnish as desired.
6. Serve warm.

NUTRITION

- Calories: 311
- Total Fat: 25.5 g
- Saturated Fat: 12.4 g
- Cholesterol: 69 mg
- Total Carbs: 1.4 g
- Fiber: 0.7 g
- Sugar: 0.3 g
- Sodium: 58 mg
- Potassium: 362 mg
- Protein: 18.4 g

PREPARATION: 10 MIN **COOKING: 6 HOURS** **SERVES: 2**

121. CHUNKY CHICKEN SALSA

INGREDIENTS

- 1 lb. chicken breast, skinless and boneless
- 1 cup chunky salsa
- 3/4 teaspoon cumin
- A pinch oregano
- Salt and black pepper to taste

DIRECTIONS

1. Start by throwing all the fixings into the Crockpot and mix them well.
2. Cover it and cook for 6 hours on Low Settings.
3. Garnish as desired.
4. Serve warm.

NUTRITION

- Calories: 541
- Total Fat: 34 g
- Saturated Fat: 8.5 g
- Cholesterol: 69 mg
- Total Carbs: 3.4 g
- Fiber: 1.2 g
- Sugar: 1 g
- Sodium: 547 mg
- Potassium: 467 mg
- Protein: 20.3 g

PREPARATION: 10 MIN **COOKING: 6 HOURS** **SERVES: 4**

122. DIJON CHICKEN

INGREDIENTS

- 2 lbs. chicken thighs, skinless and boneless
- 3/4 cup chicken stock
- 1/4 cup lemon juice
- 2 tablespoon extra virgin olive oil
- 3 tablespoon Dijon mustard
- 2 tablespoons Italian seasoning
- Salt and black pepperto taste

DIRECTIONS

1. Start by throwing all the fixings into the Crockpot and mix them well.
2. Cover it and cook for 6 hours on Low Settings.
3. Garnish as desired.
4. Serve warm.

NUTRITION

- Calories: 398
- Total Fat: 13.8 g
- Saturated Fat: 5.1 g
- Cholesterol: 200 mg
- Total Carbs: 3.6 g
- Fiber: 1 g
- Sugar: 1.3 g
- Sodium: 272 mg
- Potassium: 531 mg
- Protein: 51.8 g

PREPARATION: 10 MIN    **COOKING: 6 HOURS**   **SERVES: 6**

123. CHICKEN THIGHS WITH VEGETABLES

INGREDIENTS

- 6 chicken thighs
- 1 teaspoon vegetable oil
- 15 oz. canned tomatoes, diced
- 1 yellow onion, diced
- 2 tablespoon tomato paste
- 1/2 cup white wine
- 2 cups chicken stock
- 1 celery stalk, diced
- 1/4 lb. baby carrots, cut into halves
- 1/2 teaspoon thyme, dried
- Salt and black pepperto taste

DIRECTIONS

1. Start by throwing all the fixings into the Crockpot and mix them well.
2. Cover it and cook for 6 hours on Low Settings.
3. Shred the slow-cooked chicken using a fork and return to the pot.
4. Mix well and garnish as desired.
5. Serve warm.

NUTRITION

- Calories: 372
- Total Fat: 11.8 g
- Saturated Fat: 4.4 g
- Cholesterol: 62 mg
- Total Carbs:1.8 g
- Fiber: 0.6 g
- Sugar: 27.3 g
- Sodium: 871 mg
- Potassium: 288 mg
- Protein: 34 g

PREPARATION: 10 MIN **COOKING: 6 HOURS** **SERVES: 4**

124. CHICKEN DIPPED IN TOMATILLO SAUCE

INGREDIENTS

- 1 lb. chicken thighs, skinless and boneless
- 2 tablespoon extra virgin olive oil
- 1 yellow onion, sliced
- 1 garlic clove, crushed
- 4 oz. canned green chilies, diced
- 1 handful cilantro, diced
- 15 oz. cauliflower rice, already cooked
- 5 oz. tomatoes, diced
- 15 oz. cheddar cheese, grated
- 4 oz. black olives, pitted and diced
- Salt and black pepperto taste
- 15 oz canned tomatillos, diced

DIRECTIONS

1. Start by throwing all the fixings into the Crockpot and mix them well.
2. Cover it and cook for 5 6 hours on Low Settings.
3. Shred the slow-cooked chicken and return to the pot.
4. Mix well and garnish as desired.
5. Serve warm.

NUTRITION

- Calories: 427
- Total Fat: 31.1 g
- Saturated Fat: 4.2 g
- Cholesterol: 0 mg
- Total Carbs: 9 g
- Sugar: 12.4 g
- Fiber: 19.8 g
- Sodium: 86 mg
- Potassium: 100 mg
- Protein: 23.5 g

PREPARATION: 10 MIN   **COOKING: 3 HOURS**   **SERVES: 10**

125. CHICKEN WITH LEMON PARSLEY BUTTER

INGREDIENTS

- 1 (5 – 6lbs) whole roasting chicken, rinsed
- 1 cup water
- 1/2 teaspoon kosher salt
- 1/4 teaspoon black pepper
- 1 whole lemon, sliced
- 4 tablespoons butter
- 2 tablespoons fresh parsley, chopped

DIRECTIONS

1. Start by seasoning the chicken with all the herbs and spices.
2. Place this chicken in the Crockpot.
3. Cover it and cook for 3 hours on High Settings.
4. Meanwhile, melt butter with lemon slices and parsley in a saucepan.
5. Drizzle the butter over the Crockpot chicken.
6. Serve warm.

NUTRITION

- Calories: 379
- Total Fat: 29.7 g
- Saturated Fat: 18.6 g
- Cholesterol: 141 mg
- Total Carbs: 9.7g
- Fiber: 0.9 g
- Sugar: 1.3 g
- Sodium: 193 mg
- Potassium: 131 mg
- Protein: 25.2 g

PREPARATION: 10 MIN **COOKING: 8 HOURS** **SERVES: 8**

126. PAPRIKA CHICKEN

INGREDIENTS

- 1 free-range whole chicken
- 1 tablespoon olive oil
- 1 tablespoon dried paprika
- 1 tablespoon curry powder
- 1 teaspoon dried turmeric
- 1 teaspoon salt

DIRECTIONS

1. Start by mixing all the spices and oil in a bowl except chicken.
2. Now season the chicken with these spices liberally.
3. Add the chicken and spices to your Crockpot.
4. Cover the lid of the crockpot and cook for 8 hours on Low.
5. Serve warm.

NUTRITION

- Calories: 313
- Total Fat: 134g
- Saturated Fat: 78 g
- Cholesterol: 861 mg
- Total Carbs: 6.3 g
- Fiber: 0.7 g
- Sugar: 19 g
- Sodium: 62 mg
- Potassium: 211 mg
- Protein: 24.6 g

 **PREPARATION: 10 MIN**

 **COOKING: 8H 5 MIN**

 **SERVES: 10**

127. ROTISSERIE CHICKEN

INGREDIENTS

- 1 organic whole chicken
- 1 tablespoon olive oil
- 1 teaspoon thyme
- 1 teaspoon rosemary
- 1 teaspoon garlic, granulated
- salt and pepper

DIRECTIONS

1. Start by seasoning the chicken with all the herbs and spices.
2. Broil this seasoned chicken for 5 minutes in the oven until golden brown.
3. Place this chicken in the Crockpot.
4. Cover it and cook for 8 hours on Low Settings.
5. Serve warm.

NUTRITION

- Calories: 301
- Total Fat: 12.2 g
- Saturated: Fat 2.4 g
- Cholesterol: 110 mg
- Total Carbs: 2.5 g
- Fiber: 0.9 g
- Sugar: 1.4 g
- Sodium: 276 mg
- Potassium: 231 mg
- Protein: 28.8 g

PREPARATION: 10 MIN **COOKING: 8 HOURS** **SERVES: 6**

128. CROCKPOT CHICKEN ADOBO

INGREDIENTS

- 1/4 cup apple cider vinegar
- 12 chicken drumsticks
- 1 onion, diced into slices
- 2 tablespoons olive oil
- 10 cloves garlic, smashed
- 1 cup gluten-free tamari
- 1/4 cup diced green onion

DIRECTIONS

1. Place the drumsticks in the Crockpot and then add the remaining Ingredients: on top.
2. Cover it and cook for 8 hours on Low Settings.
3. Mix gently, then serve warm.

NUTRITION

- Calories: 249
- Total Fat: 11.9 g
- Saturated Fat: 1.7 g
- Cholesterol: 78 mg
- Total Carbs: 1.8 g
- Fiber: 1.1 g
- Sugar: 0.3 g
- Sodium: 79 mg
- Potassium: 131 mg
- Protein: 25 g

PREPARATION: 10 MIN **COOKING: 6 HOURS** **SERVES: 4**

129. CHICKEN GINGER CURRY

INGREDIENTS

- 1 ½ lbs. chicken drumsticks (approx. 5 drumsticks), skin removed
- 1 (13.5 oz.) can coconut milk
- 1 onion, diced
- 4 cloves garlic, minced
- 1-inch knob fresh ginger, minced
- 1 Serrano pepper, minced
- 1 tablespoon Garam Masala
- ½ teaspoon cayenne
- ½ teaspoon paprika
- ½ teaspoon turmeric
- salt and pepper, adjust to taste

DIRECTIONS

1. Start by throwing all the fixings into the Crockpot.
2. Cover it and cook for 6 hours on Low Settings.
3. Garnish as desired.
4. Serve warm.

NUTRITION

- Calories: 248
- Total Fat: 15.7 g
- Saturated Fat: 2.7 g
- Cholesterol: 75 mg
- Total Carbs: 8.4 g
- Fiber: 0g
- Sugar: 1.1 g
- Sodium: 94 mg
- Potassium: 331 mg
- Protein: 14.1 g

PREPARATION: 10 MIN **COOKING: 2H 30 MIN** **SERVES: 2**

130. THAI CHICKEN CURRY

INGREDIENTS

- 1 can coconut milk
- 1/2 cup chicken stock
- 1 lb. boneless, skinless chicken thighs, diced
- 1 2 tablespoons red curry paste
- 1 tablespoon coconut aminos
- 1 tablespoon fish sauce
- 2–3 garlic cloves, minced
- Salt and black pepper to taste
- red pepper flakes as desired
- 1 bag frozen mixed veggies

DIRECTIONS

1. Start by throwing all the Ingredients: except vegetables into the Crockpot.
2. Cover it and cook for 2 hours on Low Settings.
3. Remove its lid and thawed veggies.
4. Cover the crockpot again then continue cooking for another 30 minutes on Low settings.
5. Garnish as desired.
6. Serve warm.

NUTRITION

- Calories: 327
- Total Fat: 3.5 g
- Saturated Fat: 0.5 g
- Cholesterol: 162 mg
- Total Carbs: 56g
- Fiber: 0.4 g
- Sugar: 0.5 g
- Sodium: 142 mg
- Potassium: 558 mg
- Protein: 21.5 g

11. MEAT RECIPES

PREPARATION: 5 MIN

COOKING: 18 MIN

SERVES: 6

131. BEEF, PEPPER, AND GREEN BEANS STIR-FRY

INGREDIENTS

- 6 ounces ground beef
- 2 ounces chopped green bell pepper
- 4 ounces green beans
- 3 tablespoon grated cheddar cheese

Seasoning:
- ½ teaspoon salt
- ¼ teaspoon ground black pepper
- ¼ teaspoon paprika

DIRECTIONS

1. Take a skillet pan, place it over medium heat, add ground beef and cook for 4 minutes until slightly browned.
2. Then add bell pepper and green beans, season with salt, paprika, and black pepper, stir well and continue cooking for 7 to 10 minutes until beef and vegetables are fully cooked.
3. Sprinkle cheddar cheese on top, then transfer pan under the broiler and cook for 2 minutes until cheese has melted and the top is golden brown.
4. Serve.

NUTRITION

- Calories: 282.5
- Fats: 17.6g
- Protein: 26.1g
- Net carb: 2.9g
- Fiber: 2.1g

PREPARATION: 25 MIN
 COOKING: 12 MIN
 SERVES: 2

132. GARLIC STEAKS WITH ROSEMARY

INGREDIENTS

- 2 beef steaks
- 1/4 of a lime, juiced
- 1(½) teaspoon garlic powder
- ¾ teaspoon dried rosemary
- 2(½(tablespoon avocado oil

Seasoning:
- ½ teaspoon salt
- ¼ teaspoon ground black pepper

DIRECTIONS

1. Prepare steaks, and for this, sprinkle garlic powder on all sides of steak.
2. Take a shallow dish, place 1 ½ tablespoon oil and lime juice in it, whisk until combined, add steaks, turn to coat and let it marinate for 20 minutes at room temperature.
3. Then take a griddle pan, place it over medium-high heat and grease it with the remaining oil.
4. Season marinated steaks with salt and black pepper, add to the griddle pan and cook for 7 to 12 minutes until cooked to the desired level.
5. When done, wrap steaks in foil for 5 minutes, then cut into slices across the grain.
6. Sprinkle rosemary over steaks slices and then serve.

NUTRITION

- Calories: 213
- Fats: 13g
- Protein: 22g
- Net carb: 1g
- Fiber: 0g

PREPARATION: 2 MIN	**COOKING: 6 HOURS**	**SERVES: 8**

133. BALSAMIC PORK TENDERLOIN

INGREDIENTS

- 2 lb. pork tenderloin 4 minced cloves of garlic
- 1 tablespoon olive oil
- ½ c. balsamic vinegar
- 2 tablespoon coconut aminos
- 1 tablespoon Worcestershire sauce
- ½ teaspoon each: Red pepper flakes and Sea salt

DIRECTIONS

1. Drizzle the olive oil into the slow cooker. Sprinkle in the garlic, and then add the pork loin.
2. Combine the rest of the ingredients in a small container, and pour over the pork. Secure the lid on the pot and cook on low function from four to six hours or on high for three to four hours.
3. Transfer the meat to a serving platter. Pour about half of a cup of juice over the meat. Save the rest to pour over individual servings, and enjoy.

NUTRITION

- Calories: 188
- Net Carbs: 1.3 g
- Protein: 30.3 g
- Fat: 5.8 g

PREPARATION: 20 MIN

COOKING: 8 HOURS

SERVES: 16

134. CARNITAS

INGREDIENTS

- 2 tablespoon butter/bacon grease
- 1 large onion
- 4 tablespoon minced garlic
- 1 (8 lb.) Boston pork butt
- 2 tablespoon each: Chili powder, Thyme, and Cumin
- 1 tablespoon each: Pepper and Salt
- 1 c. water

DIRECTIONS

1. Grease the slow cooker with butter/oil.
2. Slice and add the onion along with the minced garlic to the pot.
3. Remove most of the fat from the meat and slice in a crisscross pattern on the top. Combine the spices, and rub the meat. (If there's any left, just add it to the top of the garlic and onions.)
4. Place the meat into the pot and add the water. Cook for eight hours (1 hr. per lb.) on the high setting.
5. It's done when it falls off the bone.

NUTRITION

- Calories: 265
- Net Carbs: 0 g
- Fat: 9 g
- Protein: 8 g

PREPARATION: 13 MIN

COOKING: 6 HOURS

SERVES: 9

135. CHILE VERDE

INGREDIENTS

- 2 lb. chopped pork stew meat
- 3 tablespoon butter/oil – divided
- 5 garlic cloves – divided – minced
- 3 tablespoon finely chopped – divided cilantro
- 1 ½ c. salsa Verde – ex. Trader Joe's
- ¼ teaspoon sea salt

For the Garnish:
- 1 tablespoon extra cilantro

DIRECTIONS

1. Warm up the slow cooker on the high setting. Add two tablespoons of the butter and melt. Toss in the cloves, and two tablespoons of the cilantro; stir. Add one tablespoon each of the garlic and cilantro.
2. Sear the pork in a skillet until just browned. Add to the cilantro garlic butter in the pot. Stir in the salsa Verde. Cover and cook for two hours on high. Lower the heat for three to four hours more (low). You may also cook on the low setting for six to eight hours.
3. Serve with some cauliflower rice or grain-free tortillas.

NUTRITION

- Calories: 206.7
- Net Carbs: 2.4 g
- Fat: 8 g
- Protein: 29 g

PREPARATION: 35 MIN

COOKING: 6 HOURS

SERVES: 12

136. CHIMICHURRI PORK ROAST

INGREDIENTS

- 2-3 lb. boneless pork roast
- Salt to taste
- 4 tablespoon extra-virgin olive oil - divided
- 1 sweet onion
- 1 lb. carrots

For the sauce
- ½ cup EVOO (olive oil)
- 3 garlic cloves
- 1 teaspoon salt
- 1 cup fresh basil/parsley leaves
- 2 tablespoon lemon juice
- ¼ teaspoon each: Ground black pepper and Cayenne pepper

DIRECTIONS

1. Place the roast in the slow cooker. Drizzle with two tablespoons of olive oil. Season with te salt and pepper. Cover the cooker, and cook on high for six hours or low for 12 hours.
2. After the pork has been in the pot for four hours on high or eight hours on low, add the onions and carrots, arranging them on each of the roast. Cook the veggies in the cooker for two more hours on high or four on the low setting.
3. Make the Sauce: Combine all of the ingredients in a blender until the basil is in small bits.
4. Pull the roast apart and place the veggies on a serving platter. Pour the sauce and enjoy.

NUTRITION

- Calories: 167
- Net Carbs: 5.0 g
- Fat: 8.0 g
- Protein: 17 g

PREPARATION: 15 MIN **COOKING: 8 HOURS** **SERVES: 10**

137. GINGER & LIME PORK

INGREDIENTS

- Salt and pepper to taste
- 1 tablespoon olive/ avocado oil
- 1teaspoon stevia drops - vanilla
- 2 ½ lbs. pork loin
- 2 tablespoon low-carb brown sugar/molasses substitute
- 1/4 cup tamari
- 1 tablespoon Worcestershire sauce
- Juice of one lemon
- 1 tablespoon fresh ginger/½teaspoon ground
- ½teaspoon xanthan gum
- Optional: Fresh cilantro

DIRECTIONS

1. Prepare a large skillet on the stovetop with the oil.
2. Rub the pepper and salt over the pork loin, and place it in hot oil in the skillet. Sear all sides until browned.
3. Take it from the burner, and place it in the bottom of the slow cooker.
4. Whisk together the ginger, garlic, lime juice, Worcestershire sauce, sweeteners, and tamarin. Pour the mixture over the pork loin.
5. Place a cover on top of the slow cooker. Program the pork on high for four to seven hours or six hours on low. When finished arrange the pork on a platter and for the dishes in a small saucepan. sprinkle day xanthan gum on top. With the powder in and cook until the mixture has thickened. Pour over the loin and garnish with some fresh cilantro.

NUTRITION

- Calories: 292
- Net Carbs: 1.9 g
- Fat: 16 g
- Protein: 31.9 g

PREPARATION: 20 MIN

COOKING: 9 HOURS

SERVES: 12

138. KALUA PORK & CABBAGE

INGREDIENTS

- 1 boneless (approx. 3 lb.) pork shoulder butt roast
- 1 med. head of cabbage (approx. 2 lb.)
- 7 strips bacon – divided
- 1 tablespoon coarse sea salt

DIRECTIONS

1. Coarsely chop the cabbage. Trim the fat from the roast.
2. Layer most of the bacon in the cooker. Dust the salt over the roast and add to the slow cooker on top of the bacon. Place the remaining bacon on top. Close the top, and cook on low for eight to ten hours.
3. At that time, drop in the cabbage on top, and continue cooking covered for another hour until the cabbage is tender. (It may take a little longer depending on the size of the cooker.
4. When the roast is completed, remove and shred. Use a slotted spoon to arrange the cabbage in the serving dish.
5. Use some of the slow cooker juices on the side for dipping.

NUTRITION

- Calories: 227
- Net Carbs: 4 g
- Fat: 13 g
- Protein: 22 g

PREPARATION: 30 MIN **COOKING: 4 HOURS** **SERVES: 2**

139. PORK HOCK

INGREDIENTS

- 1 lb. pork hock
- 1/3 cup each: Soy sauce and Shaoxing cooking wine
- ¼ cup each: Rice vinegar, Soy sauce, and Splenda/ another favorite keto sweetener
- ½ cup shiitake mushrooms
- 1/3 med. onion
- 2 crushed cloves of garlic
- 1 teaspoon each: Chinese five-spice and Oregano
- 1 tablespoon butter

DIRECTIONS

1. Warm up the slow cooker using the high heat setting.
2. Arrange the onions in a skillet to fry. Fill up another saucepan with water to boil the mushrooms.
3. Also, set up a pan to sear the hock using the butter. Brown the hock in the butter until crispy.
4. Toss in all of the ingredients into the slow cooker, mixing well. Let it cook in the high setting for two hours. Stir and continue cooking for another two hours in the low heat setting.
5. Transfer the pork from the cooker and debone. Slice and add it back to the sauce. Stir and serve with a favorite side dish.

NUTRITION

- Calories: 530
- Net Carbs: 6.37 g
- Fat: 31.4 g
- Protein: 20.81 g

PREPARATION: 45 MIN **COOKING: 6 HOURS** **SERVES: 8**

140. PULLED PORK

INGREDIENTS

- 1 large white onion
- 3 bay leaves
- 3 ½ lb. pork shoulder
- 1/3 cup spicy chocolate barbecue sauce
- Spices for Rub
- 1 tablespoon of each: Garlic powder, Paprika, Onion powder, and Smoked paprika
- ½ teaspoon white or black pepper

DIRECTIONS

1. Set the temperature on your slow cooker to high.
2. Combine all of the spices in a mixing bowl. Use a sharp knife to score the skin of the pork approximately one-inch apart—going in both directions making it appear to have square cuts.
3. Rub the spices into the pork. Peel and crudely chop the onions, adding them to the slow cooker along with the bay leaves.
4. Arrange the pork on top and cover with the lid. Cook on low for 8 to 10 hours or high for five to six hours. It all depends on the size cooker you use.
5. When the pork is done, open the top and let the steam out. If you like a crispy top, preheat the oven temperature to 400°F.
6. Use two forks to transfer the pork onto the baking sheet that should be lined with parchment paper.
7. Use the barbecue sauce to cover the entire surface of the pork, and place it in the oven. Cook 30 to 40 minutes or until wanted brownness is accomplished.
8. Prepare the sauce. Combine the liquid with the cooked onions and bay leaves into a blender. Mix until smooth.
9. Remove the pork from the oven when done, and place it in a bowl.
10. Shred the meat bits, and pour the sauce from the blender over the top, and stir well.
11. Serve right away and enjoy with some roasted veggies.

NUTRITION

- Calories: 497
- Net Carbs: 3.8 g
- Fat: 36.6 g
- Protein: 35.0 g

PREPARATION: 5 MIN **COOKING: 4 HOURS** **SERVES: 8**

141. SPICY PORK CHOPS

INGREDIENTS

- 1 teaspoon salt
- 1 tablespoon each:
- Dried thyme
- Dried curry powder
- Ground cumin
- Fennel seeds
- Freshly chopped chives
- Dried rosemary
- 2 lb. pork chops
- 4 tablespoon olive oil

DIRECTIONS

1. Mix all of the spices with ½ of the oil. Use the prepared rub to cover the chops.
2. Dump the remainder of the olive oil into the slow cooker. Arrange the meat in the pot. Cover with the top. Select either four hours using the high setting or cook eight hours on low.

NUTRITION

- Calories: 247
- Net Carbs: 1 g
- Fat: 15 g
- Protein: 24 g

PREPARATION: 25 MIN **COOKING: 6 HOURS** **SERVES: 12**

142. LAMB BARBACOA

INGREDIENTS

- ¼ cup dried mustard
- 5 ½ lbs. leg of lamb - boneless
- 2 tablespoon each:
- Smoked paprika
- Himalayan salt
- 1 tablespoon each:
- Chipotle powder
- Dried oregano
- Ground cumin
- 1 cup water

DIRECTIONS

1. Combine the chipotle powder, oregano, cumin, paprika, and salt.
2. Cover the roast with the dried mustard, and sprinkle with the prepared spices.
3. Arrange the lamb in the slow cooker, cover, and let it marinate in the refrigerator overnight.
4. Once you're ready to cook, just add one cup of water to the slow cooker on the high heat setting. Cook for six hours.
5. When done, remove all except for one cup of the cooking juices, and shred the lamb. Using the rest of the cooking juices—adjust the seasoning as you desire.

NUTRITION

- Calories: 492
- Net Carbs: 1.2 g
- Fat: 35.8 g
- Protein: 37.5 g

PREPARATION: 5 MIN

COOKING: 6-10 HOURS

SERVES: 4

143. LAMB WITH MINT & GREEN BEANS

INGREDIENTS

- ½teaspoon salt – Himalayan pink
- Freshly cracked black pepper
- 1 lamb leg – bone-in
- 2 tablespoon lard/ghee/tallow
- 4 garlic cloves
- 6 cup trimmed green beans
- ¼ freshly chopped mint/1-2 tablespoon dried mint

DIRECTIONS

1. Warm up the slow cooker with the high setting.
2. Paper towel dry the lamp. Sprinkle with pepper and salt. Grease a Dutch oven or similar large pot with the ghee/lard.
3. Sear the lamb until golden brown, and set aside.
4. Remove the peels from the garlic and mince. Dice up the mint.
5. Arrange the seared lamb in the cooker, and give it a shake of the garlic and mint.
6. Note: You can add ½ cup to one cup of water to the cooker if it gets dried out. Secure the lid and program the cooker on the low heat function for 10 hours or on the high function for 6 hours.
7. After about four hours, switch the lamb out of the cooker. Toss in the green beans and return the lamb back into the pot.
8. Let the flavors mingle for about two more hours. The meat should be tender and the beans crispy.
9. Serve and enjoy!

NUTRITION

- Calories: 525
- Net Carbs: 7.6 g
- Protein: 37.3 g
- Fat: 36.4 g

PREPARATION: 15 MIN   **COOKING: 9 HOURS**   **SERVES: 12**

144. TARRAGON LAMB SHANK & BEANS

INGREDIENTS

- 4 (1 ½ lb.) lamb shanks
- 1 can (19 Oz.) white beans/ cannellini- for example
- 1 ½ cup peeled - diced carrot
- 2 thinly sliced garlic cloves
- 1 cup chopped onion
- ¾ cup chopped celery
- 2 teaspoons dried tarragon
- ¼ teaspoon freshly cracked black pepper
- 2 teaspons dried tarragon
- 1 can (28 oz.) diced tomatoes - not drained

DIRECTIONS

1. Remove all of the fat from the lamb shanks. Pour the beans, cloves of garlic, carrots, celery, and onion into the cooker.
2. Arrange the shanks on top of the beans, and sprinkle with the salt, pepper, and tarragon. Empty the tomatoes over the lamb - including the juices. Cover and cook the lamb on high for approximately one hour.
3. Lower the heat to the low setting, and cook for nine hours or until the lamb is tender.
4. Take the lamb out of the slow cooker, and set it aside. Empty the bean mixture through a colander over a bowl to reserve the liquid. Let the juices stand for five minutes and skim off the fat from the surface.
5. Return the bean mixture to the liquid in the slow cooker. Strip the lamb bones, and throw the bones away. Serve with the bean mixture, and enjoy with your family and friends.

NUTRITION

- Calories: 353
- Net Carbs: 12.9 g
- Fat: 16.3 g
- Protein: 50.3 g

PREPARATION: 20 MIN **COOKING: 8 HOURS** **SERVES: 6**

145. TASTY & EASY LAMB

INGREDIENTS

- ¼ cup dried mustard
- 5 ½ lbs. leg of lamb - boneless

2 tablespoon each:
- Smoked paprika
- Himalayan salt

1 tablespoon each:
- Chipotle powder
- Dried oregano
- Ground cumin
- 1 cup water

DIRECTIONS

1. Combine the chipotle powder, oregano, cumin, paprika, and salt.
2. Cover the roast with the dried mustard, and sprinkle with the prepared spices.
3. Arrange the lamb in the slow cooker, cover, and let it marinate in the refrigerator overnight.
4. Once you're ready to cook, just add one cup of water to the slow cooker on the high heat setting. Cook for six hours.
5. When done, remove all except for one cup of the cooking juices, and shred the lamb. Using the rest of the cooking juices—adjust the seasoning as you desire.

NUTRITION

- Calories: 492
- Net Carbs: 1.2 g
- Fat: 35.8 g
- Protein: 37.5 g

12. SEAFOOD RECIPES

PREPARATION: 10 MIN

COOKING: 12 MIN

SERVES: 2

146. BACON-WRAPPED MAHI-MAHI

INGREDIENTS

- 2 fillets of mahi-mahi
- 2 strips of bacon
- ½ of lime, zested
- 4 basil leaves
- ½ teaspoon salt

Seasoning:
- ½ teaspoon ground black pepper
- 1 tablespoon avocado oil

DIRECTIONS

1. Turn on the oven, then set it to 375°F and let them preheat.
2. Meanwhile, season fillets with salt and black pepper, top each fillet with 2 basil leaves, sprinkle with lime zest, wrap with a bacon strip and secure with a toothpick if needed.
3. Take a medium skillet pan, place it over medium-high heat, add oil and when hot, place prepared fillets in it and cook for 2 minutes per side.
4. Transfer pan into the oven and bake the fish for 5 to 7 minutes until thoroughly cooked.
5. Serve.

NUTRITION

- Calories: 217
- Fats: 11.3g
- Protein: 27.1g
- Net carbs: 1.2g
- Fiber: 0.5g

PREPARATION: 10 MIN

COOKING: 15 MIN

SERVES: 2

147. GARLIC BUTTER SALMON

INGREDIENTS

- 2 salmon fillets, skinless
- 1 teaspoon minced garlic
- 1 tablespoon chopped cilantro
- 1 tablespoon unsalted butter
- 2 tablespoon grated cheddar cheese

Seasoning:
- ½ teaspoon salt
- ¼ teaspoon ground black pepper

DIRECTIONS

1. Turn on the oven, then set it to 350°F, and let it preheat.
2. Meanwhile, taking a rimmed baking sheet, grease it with oil, place salmon fillets on it, season with salt and black pepper on both sides.
3. Stir together butter, cilantro, and cheese until combined, then coat the mixture on both sides of salmon in an even layer and bake for 15 minutes until thoroughly cooked.
4. Then turn on the broiler and continue baking the salmon for 2 minutes until the top is golden brown.
5. Serve.

NUTRITION

- Calories: 128
- Fats: 4.5g
- Protein: 41g
- Net carb: 1g
- Fiber: 0g

PREPARATION: 10 MIN

COOKING: 20 MIN

SERVES: 2

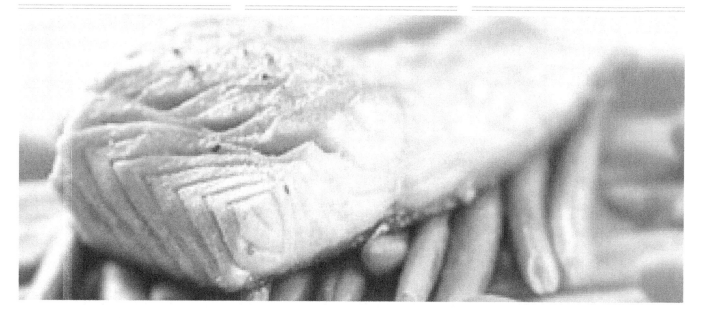

148. SALMON WITH GREEN BEANS

INGREDIENTS

- 6 ounces green beans
- 3 ounces unsalted butter
- 2 salmon fillets

Seasoning:
- ½ teaspoon garlic powder
- ½ teaspoon salt
- ½ teaspoon cracked black pepper

DIRECTIONS

1. Take a frying pan, place butter in it and when it starts to melts, add beans and salmon in fillets in it, season with garlic powder, salt, and black pepper, and cook for 8 minutes until salmon is cooked, turning halfway through and stirring the beans frequently.
2. When done, evenly divide salmon and green beans between two plates and serve.

NUTRITION

- Calories: 352
- Fats: 29g
- Protein: 19g
- Net carb: 3.5g
- Fiber: 1.5g

PREPARATION: 10 MIN

COOKING: 20 MIN

SERVES: 2

149. SALMON SHEET PAN

INGREDIENTS

- 2 salmon fillets
- 2 ounces cauliflower florets
- 2 ounces broccoli florets
- 1 teaspoon minced garlic
- 1 tablespoon chopped cilantro

Seasoning:
- 2 tablespoon coconut oil
- 2/3 teaspoon salt
- ¼ teaspoon ground black pepper

DIRECTIONS

1. Turn on the oven, then set it to 400°F, and let it preheat.
2. Place oil in a small bowl, add garlic and cilantro, stir well, and microwave for 1 minute or until the oil has melted.
3. Take a rimmed baking sheet, place cauliflower and broccoli florets in it, drizzle with 1 tablespoon of coconut oil mixture, season with 1/3 teaspoon salt, 1/8 teaspoon black pepper, and bake for 10 minutes.
4. Then push the vegetables to a side, place salmon fillets in the pan, drizzle with the remaining coconut oil mixture, season with the remaining salt and black pepper on both sides and bake for 10 minutes until salmon is fork-tender.
5. Serve.

NUTRITION

- Calories: 450
- Fats: 23.8g
- Protein: 36.9g
- Net carb: 5.9g
- Fiber: 2.g

PREPARATION: 5 MIN **COOKING: 10 MIN** **SERVES: 2**

150. BACON-WRAPPED SALMON

INGREDIENTS

- 2 salmon fillets, cut into four pieces
- 4 slices of bacon
- 2 teaspoon avocado oil
- 2 tablespoon mayonnaise

Seasoning:
- ½ teaspoon salt
- ½ teaspoon ground black pepper

DIRECTIONS

1. Turn on the oven, then set it to 375°F and let it preheat.
2. Meanwhile, place a skillet pan, place it over medium-high heat, add oil and let it heat.
3. Season salmon fillets with salt and black pepper, wrap each salmon fillet with a bacon slice, then add to the pan and cook for 4 minutes, turning halfway through.
4. Then transfer skillet pan containing salmon into the oven and cook salmon for 5 minutes until thoroughly cooked.
5. Serve salmon with mayonnaise.

NUTRITION

- Calories: 190.7
- Fats: 16.5g
- Protein: 10.5g
- Net Carb: 0g
- Fiber: 0g

PREPARATION: 5 MIN   **COOKING: 15 MIN**   **SERVES: 4**

151. STIR-FRY TUNA WITH VEGETABLES

INGREDIENTS

- 4 ounces tuna, packed in water
- 2 ounces broccoli florets
- ½ red bell pepper, cored, sliced
- ½ teaspoon minced garlic
- ½ teaspoon sesame seeds

Seasoning:
- 1 tablespoon avocado oil
- 2/3 teaspoon soy sauce
- 2/3 teaspoon apple cider vinegar
- 3 tablespoon water

DIRECTIONS

1. Take a skillet pan, add ½ tablespoon oil and when hot, add bell pepper and cook for 3 minutes until tender-crisp.
2. Then add broccoli floret, drizzle with water and continue cooking for 3 minutes until steamed, covering the pan.
3. Uncover the pan, cook for 2 minutes until all the liquid has evaporated, and then push bell pepper to one side of the pan.
4. Add the remaining oil to the other side of the pan, add tuna and cook for 3 minutes until seared on all sides.
5. Then drizzle with soy sauce and vinegar, toss all the ingredients in the pan until mixed and sprinkle with sesame seeds.
6. Serve.

NUTRITION

- Calories: 99.7
- Fats: 5.1g
- Protein: 11g
- Net carb: 1.6g
- Fiber: 1g

PREPARATION: 5 MIN

COOKING: 10 MIN

SERVES: 2

152. CHILI-GLAZED SALMON

INGREDIENTS

- 2 salmon fillets
- 2 tablespoon sweet chili sauce
- 2 teaspoon chopped chives
- ½ teaspoon sesame seeds

DIRECTIONS

1. Turn on the oven, then set it to 400°F and let it preheat.
2. Meanwhile, place salmon in a shallow dish, add chili sauce and chives and toss until mixed.
3. Transfer prepared salmon onto a baking sheet lined with parchment sheet, drizzle with the remaining sauce and bake for 10 minutes until thoroughly cooked.
4. Garnish with sesame seeds and serve.

NUTRITION

- Calories: 112.5
- Fats: 5.6g
- Protein: 12g
- Net carb: 3.4g
- Fiber: 0g

PREPARATION: 5 MIN

COOKING: 20 MIN

SERVES: 2

153. CARDAMOM SALMON

INGREDIENTS

- 2 salmon fillets
- ¾ teaspoon salt
- 2/3 tablespoon ground cardamom
- 1 tablespoon liquid stevia
- 1(½) tablespoon avocado oil

DIRECTIONS

1. Turn on the oven, then set it to 275°F and let it preheat.
2. Meanwhile, prepare the sauce and for this, place oil in a small bowl, and whisk in cardamom and stevia until combined.
3. Take a baking dish, place salmon in it, brush with prepared sauce on all sides, and let it marinate for 20 minutes at room temperature.
4. Then season salmon with salt and bake for 15 to 20 minutes until it is cooked.
5. When done, flake salmon with two forks and then serve.

NUTRITION

- Calories: 143.3
- Fats: 10.7g
- Protein: 118.g
- Net carb: 0g
- Fiber: 0g

PREPARATION: 5 MIN

COOKING: 0 MIN

SERVES: 2

154. CREAMY TUNA, SPINACH, AND EGGS PLATES

INGREDIENTS

- 2 ounces spinach leaves
- 2 ounces tuna, packed in water
- 2 eggs, boiled
- 4 tablespoon cream cheese, full-fat

Seasoning:
- ¼ teaspoon salt
- 1/8 teaspoon ground black pepper

DIRECTIONS

1. Take two plates and evenly distribute spinach and tuna between them.
2. Peel the eggs, cut them into half, and divide them between the plates and then season with salt and black pepper.
3. Serve with cream cheese.

NUTRITION

- Calories: 212
- Fats: 14.1g
- Protein: 18g
- Net carb: 3.5g
- Fiber: 1.5g

PREPARATION: 5 MIN

COOKING: 0 MIN

SERVES: 2

155. TUNA AND AVOCADO

INGREDIENTS

- 2 ounces tuna, packed in water
- 1 avocado, pitted
- 8 green olives
- ½ cup mayonnaise, full-fat

Seasoning:
- 1/3 teaspoon salt
- 1/4 teaspoon ground black pepper

DIRECTIONS

1. Cut avocado into half, then remove the pit, scoop out the flesh and distribute between two plates.
2. Add tuna and green olives and then season with salt and black pepper.
3. Serve with mayonnaise.

NUTRITION

- Calories: 680
- Fats: 65.6g
- Protein: 10.2g
- Net carb: 2.2g
- Fiber: 2.4g

PREPARATION: 5 MIN

COOKING: 15 MIN

SERVES: 2

156. BAKED FISH WITH FETA AND TOMATO

INGREDIENTS

- 2 pacific whitening fillets
- 1 scallion, chopped
- 1 Roma tomato, chopped
- 1 teaspoon fresh oregano
- 1-ounce feta cheese, crumbled

Seasoning:
- 2 tablespoon avocado oil
- 1/3 teaspoon salt
- 1/4 teaspoon ground black pepper
- ¼ crushed red pepper

DIRECTIONS

1. Turn on the oven, then set it to 400°F and let it preheat.
2. Take a medium skillet pan, place it over medium heat, add oil and when hot, add scallion and cook for 3 minutes.
3. Add tomatoes, stir in ½ teaspoon oregano, 1/8 teaspoon salt, black pepper, red pepper, pour in ¼ cup water and bring it to simmer.
4. Sprinkle the remaining salt over fillets, add to the pan, drizzle with the remaining oil, and then bake for 10 to 12 minutes until fillets are fork-tender.
5. When done, top fish with the remaining oregano and cheese and then serve.

NUTRITION

- Calories: 427.5
- Fats: 29.5g
- Protein: 26.7g
- Net carb: 8g
- Fiber: 4g

13. SNACK RECIPES

PREPARATION: 5 MIN

COOKING: 25 MIN

SERVES: 2

157. BLUEBERRY SCONES

INGREDIENTS

- 2 cups almond flour
- 1/3 cup Swerve sweetener
- ¼ cup coconut flour
- 1 tablespoon baking powder
- ¼ teaspoon salt
- 2 large eggs
- ¼ cup heavy whipping cream
- ½ teaspoon vanilla extract
- ¾ cup fresh blueberries

DIRECTIONS

1. Preheat your oven at 325°F. Layer a baking sheet with wax paper.
2. Whisk almond flour with baking powder, salt, coconut flour, and sweetener in a large bowl.
3. Stir in eggs, vanilla, and cream then mix well until fully incorporated.
4. Add blueberries and mix gently.
5. Spread this dough on a baking sheet and form it into a 10x8-inch rectangle.
6. Bake these scones for 25 minutes until golden.
7. Allow them to cool then serve.

NUTRITION

- Calories: 266
- Fat: 25.7g
- Saturated fat: 1.2g
- Cholesterol: 41g
- Sodium: 18g

PREPARATION: 5 MIN

COOKING: 30 MIN

SERVES: 12

158. HOMEMADE GRAHAM CRACKERS

INGREDIENTS

- 2 cups almond flour
- 1/3 cup Swerve Brown
- 2 teaspoon cinnamon
- 1 teaspoon baking powder
- Pinch salt
- 1 large egg
- 2 tablespoon butter, melted
- 1 teaspoon vanilla extract

DIRECTIONS

1. Preheat your oven at 300°F.
2. Whisk almond flour, baking powder, salt, cinnamon, and sweetener in a large bowl.
3. Stir in melted butter, egg, and vanilla extract.
4. Mix well to form the dough, then spread it out into a ¼-inch thick sheet.
5. Slice the sheet into 2x2-inch squares and place them on a baking sheet with wax paper.
6. Bake them for 30 minutes until golden, then let them sit for 30 minutes at room temperature until cooled.
7. Break the crackers into smaller squares and put them back in the hot oven for 30 minutes. Keep the oven off during this time.
8. Enjoy.

NUTRITION

- Calories: 243
- Fat: 21g
- Cholesterol: 121g
- Sodium: 34g
- Carbohydrates: 7.3g
- Protein: 4.3g

PREPARATION: 5 MIN

COOKING: 25 MIN

SERVES: 2

159. BUFFALO CHICKEN SAUSAGE BALLS

INGREDIENTS

- 2 14-ox sausages, casings removed
- 2 cups almond flour
- 1 ½ cups shredded cheddar cheese
- ½ cup crumbled blue cheese
- 1 teaspoon salt
- ½ teaspoon pepper

Blue cheese ranch dipping sauce:
- 1/3 cup mayonnaise
- 1/3 cup almond milk, unsweetened
- 2 cloves garlic, minced
- 1 teaspoon dried dill
- ½ teaspoon dried parsley
- ½ teaspoon salt
- ½ teaspoon pepper
- ¼ cup crumbled blue cheese (or more, if desired)

DIRECTIONS

1. Preheat your oven at 350°F.
2. Layer two baking sheets with wax paper and set them aside.
3. Mix sausage with cheddar cheese, almond flour, salt, pepper, and bleu cheese in a large bowl.
4. Make 1-inch balls out of this mixture and place them on the baking sheets.
5. Bake them for 25 minutes until golden brown.
6. Meanwhile, prepare the dipping sauce by whisking all of its ingredients in a bowl.
7. Serve the balls with this dipping sauce.

NUTRITION

- Calories: 183
- Fat: 15g
- Cholesterol 11mg
- Sodium 31mg
- Total carbohydrates 6.2g
- Protein 4.5g

PREPARATION: 5 MIN	**COOKING: 15 MIN**	**SERVES: 6**

160. BRUSSELS SPROUTS CHIPS

INGREDIENTS

- 1-pound Brussels sprouts, washed and dried
- 2 tablespoon extra-virgin olive oil
- 1 teaspoon kosher salt

DIRECTIONS

1. Preheat your oven at 400°F.
2. After peeling the sprouts off the stem, discard the outer leaves of the Brussels sprouts.
3. Separate all the leaves from one another and place them on a baking sheet.
4. Toss them with oil and salt thoroughly to coat them well.
5. Spread the leaves out on two greased baking sheets, then bake them for 15 minutes until crispy.
6. Serve.

NUTRITION

- Calories: 188
- Fat: 3g
- Cholesterol: 101mg
- Sodium: 54mg
- Fiber: 0.6g
- Protein: 5g

PREPARATION: 5 MIN

COOKING: 0 MIN

SERVES: 2

161. KETO CHOCOLATE MOUSSE

INGREDIENTS

- 1 cup heavy whipping cream
- ¼ cup unsweetened cocoa powder, sifted
- ¼ cup Swerve powdered sweetener
- 1 teaspoon vanilla extract
- ¼ teaspoon kosher salt

DIRECTIONS

1. Add cream to the bowl of an electric stand mixture and beat it until it forms peaks.
2. Stir in cocoa powder, vanilla, sweetener, and salt.
3. Mix well until smooth.
4. Refrigerate for 4 hours.
5. Serve.

NUTRITION

- Calories: 153
- Fat: 13g
- Cholesterol: 6.5mg
- Sodium: 81mg
- Sugar: 1.4g
- Protein: 5.8g

 **PREPARATION: 5 MIN**	 **COOKING: 0 MIN**	 **SERVES: 2**

162. KETO BERRY MOUSSE

INGREDIENTS

- 2 cups heavy whipping cream
- 3 ounces fresh raspberries
- 2 ounces chopped pecans
- ½ lemon, zested
- ¼ teaspoon vanilla extract

DIRECTIONS

1. Beat cream in a bowl using a hand mixer until it forms peaks.
2. Stir in vanilla and lemon zest and mix well until incorporated.
3. Fold in nuts and berries and mix well.
4. Cover the mixture with plastic wrap and refrigerate for 3 hours.
5. Serve fresh.

NUTRITION

- Calories: 254
- Fat: 9g
- Cholesterol: 13mg
- Sodium: 179mg
- Sugar: 1.2g
- Protein: 7.5g

 **PREPARATION: 5 MIN**  **COOKING: 0 MIN**  **SERVES: 4**

163. PEANUT BUTTER MOUSSE

INGREDIENTS

- ½ cup heavy whipping cream
- 4 ounces cream cheese, softened
- ¼ cup natural peanut butter
- ¼ cup powdered Swerve sweetener
- ½ teaspoon vanilla extract
- Pinch of salt

DIRECTIONS

1. Beat ½ cup cream in a medium bowl with a hand mixer until it forms peaks.
2. Beat cream cheese with peanut butter in another bowl until creamy.
3. Stir in vanilla, a pinch of salt, and sweetener to the peanut butter mix and combine until smooth.
4. Fold in the prepared whipped cream and mix well until fully incorporated.
5. Divide the mousse into 4 serving glasses.
6. Garnish as desired.
7. Enjoy.

NUTRITION

- Calories: 290
- Fat: 21.5g
- Cholesterol: 12g
- Sodium: 9g
- Protein: 6g

PREPARATION: 10 MIN

COOKING: 120 MIN

SERVES: 2

164. COOKIE ICE CREAM

INGREDIENTS

Cookie crumbs:
- ¾ cup almond flour
- ¼ cup cocoa powder
- ¼ teaspoon baking soda
- ¼ cup erythritol
- ½ teaspoon vanilla extract
- 1 ½ tablespoon coconut oil, softened
- 1 large egg, room temperature
- Pinch of salt

Ice cream:
- 2 ½ cups whipping cream
- 1 tablespoon vanilla extract
- ½ cup erythritol
- ½ cup almond milk, unsweetened

DIRECTIONS

1. Preheat your oven at 300°F and layer a 9-inch baking pan with wax paper.
2. Whisk almond flour with baking soda, cocoa powder, salt, and erythritol in a medium bowl.
3. Stir in coconut oil and vanilla extract, then mix well until crumbly.
4. Whisk in egg and mix well to form the dough.
5. Spread this dough in the prepared pan and bake for 20 minutes in the preheated oven.
6. Allow the crust to cool, then crush it finely into crumbles.
7. Beat cream in a large bowl with a hand mixer until it forms a stiff peak.
8. Stir in erythritol and vanilla extract, then mix well until fully incorporated.
9. Pour in milk and blend well until smooth.
10. Add this mixture to an ice cream machine and churn as per the machine's instructions.
11. Add cookie crumbles to the ice cream in the machine and churn again.
12. Place the ice cream in a sealable container and freeze for 2 hours.
13. Scoop out the ice cream and serve.
14. Enjoy.
15. Note: this recipe calls for an ice cream machine

NUTRITION

- Calories: 214
- Fat: 19g
- Cholesterol: 15g
- Sodium: 12g
- Fiber: 2g
- Protein: 7g

PREPARATION: 10 MIN **COOKING: 0 MIN** **SERVES: 2**

165. MOCHA ICE CREAM

INGREDIENTS

- 1 cup coconut milk
- ¼ cup heavy whipping cream
- 2 tablespoon erythritol
- 15 drops liquid stevia
- 2 tablespoon unsweetened cocoa powder
- 1 tablespoon instant coffee
- ¼ teaspoon xanthan gum

DIRECTIONS

1. Whisk everything except xanthan gum in a bowl using a hand mixer.
2. Slowly add xanthan gum and stir well to make a thick mixture.
3. Churn the mixture in an ice cream machine as per the machine's instructions.
4. Freeze it for 2 hours, then garnish with mint and instant coffee.
5. Serve.
6. Note: this recipe calls for an ice cream machine

NUTRITION

- Calories: 267
- Fat: 44.5g
- Cholesterol: 153mg
- Sodium: 217mg

 **PREPARATION: 10 MIN**

 **COOKING: 0 MIN**

 **SERVES: 2**

166. RASPBERRY CREAM FAT BOMBS

INGREDIENTS

- 1 packet raspberry Jello (sugar-free)
- 1 teaspoon gelatin powder
- ½ cup of boiling water
- ½ cup heavy cream

DIRECTIONS

1. Mix Jello and gelatin in boiling water in a medium bowl.
2. Stir in cream slowly and mix it for 1 minute.
3. Divide this mixture into candy molds.
4. Refrigerate them for 30 minutes.
5. Enjoy.

NUTRITION

- Calories: 197
- Fat: 19.2g
- Cholesterol: 11mg
- Sodium: 78mg

PREPARATION: 10 MIN **COOKING: 50 MIN** **SERVES: 2**

167. CAULIFLOWER TARTAR BREAD

INGREDIENTS

- 3 cup cauliflower rice
- 10 large eggs, yolks and egg whites separated
- ¼ teaspoon cream of tartar
- 1(¼) cup coconut flour
- 1(½) tablespoon gluten-free baking powder
- 1 teaspoon sea salt
- 6 tablespoon butter
- 6 cloves garlic, minced
- 1 tablespoon fresh rosemary, chopped
- 1 tablespoon fresh parsley, chopped

DIRECTIONS

1. Preheat your oven to 350°F. Layer a 9x5-inch pan with wax paper.
2. Place the cauliflower rice in a suitable bowl and then cover it with plastic wrap.
3. Heat it for 4 minutes in the microwave. Heat more if the cauliflower isn't soft enough.
4. Place the cauliflower rice in a kitchen towel and squeeze it to drain excess water.
5. Transfer drained cauliflower rice to a food processor.
6. Add coconut flour, sea salt, baking powder, butter, egg yolks, and garlic. Blend until crumbly.
7. Beat egg whites with cream of tartar in a bowl until foamy.
8. Add egg white mixture to the cauliflower mixture and stir well with a spatula.
9. Fold in rosemary and parsley.
10. Spread this batter in the prepared baking pan evenly.
11. Bake it for 50 minutes until golden, then allow it to cool.

NUTRITION

- Calories: 104
- Fat: 8.9g
- Cholesterol: 57mg
- Sodium: 340mg
- Carbohydrates: 4.7g

 **PREPARATION: 10 MIN**  **COOKING: 10 MIN**  **SERVES: 4**

168. BUTTERY SKILLET FLATBREAD

INGREDIENTS

- 1 cup almond flour
- 2 tablespoon coconut flour
- 2 teaspoon xanthan gum
- ½ teaspoon baking powder
- ½ teaspoon salt
- 1 whole egg + 1 egg white
- 1 tablespoon water (if needed)
- 1 tablespoon oil, for frying
- 1 tablespoon melted butter, for brushing

DIRECTIONS

1. Mix xanthan gum with flours, salt, and baking powder in a suitable bowl.
2. Beat egg and egg white in a separate bowl, then stir in the flour mixture.
3. Mix well until smooth. Add a tablespoon of water if the dough is too thick.
4. Place a large skillet over medium heat and heat oil.

NUTRITION

- Calories: 272
- Fat: 18g
- Cholesterol: 6.1g

PREPARATION: 20 MIN **COOKING: 60 MIN** **SERVES: 2**

169. FLUFFY BITES

INGREDIENTS

- 2 teaspoons cinnamon
- 2/3 cup sour cream
- 2 cups heavy cream
- 1 teaspoon scraped vanilla bean
- ¼ teaspoon cardamom
- 4 egg yolks
- Stevia to taste

DIRECTIONS

1. Start by whisking your egg yolks until creamy and smooth.
2. Get out a double boiler, and add your eggs with the rest of your ingredients. Mix well.
3. Remove from heat, allowing it to cool until it reaches room temperature.
4. Refrigerate for an hour before whisking well.
5. Pour into molds, and freeze for at least an hour before serving.

NUTRITION

- Calories: 363
- Protein: 2g
- Fat: 40g
- Carbohydrates: 1g

PREPARATION: 20 MIN   **COOKING: 60 MIN**   **SERVES: 12**

170. COCONUT FUDGE

INGREDIENTS

- 2 cups coconut oil
- ½ cup dark cocoa powder
- ½ cup coconut cream
- ¼ cup almonds, chopped
- ¼ cup coconut, shredded
- 1 teaspoon almond extract
- Pinch of salt
- Stevia to taste

DIRECTIONS

1. Pour your coconut oil and coconut cream in a bowl, whisking with an electric beater until smooth. Once the mixture becomes smooth and glossy, do not continue.
2. Begin to add in your cocoa powder while mixing slowly, making sure that there aren't any lumps.
3. Add the rest of your ingredients, and mix well.
4. Line a bread pan with parchment paper, and freeze until it sets.
5. Slice into squares before serving.

NUTRITION

- Calories: 172
- Fat: 20g
- Carbohydrates: 3g

PREPARATION: 30 MIN | **COOKING: 60 MIN** | **SERVES: 12**

171. NUTMEG NOUGAT

INGREDIENTS

- 1 cup heavy cream
- 1 cup cashew butter
- 1 cup coconut, shredded
- ½ teaspoon nutmeg
- 1 teaspoon vanilla extract, pure
- Stevia to taste

DIRECTIONS

1. Melt your cashew butter using a double boiler, and then stir in your vanilla extract, dairy cream, nutmeg, and stevia. Make sure it's mixed well.
2. Remove from heat, allowing it to cool down before refrigerating it for a half-hour.
3. Shape into balls, and coat with shredded coconut. Chill for at least two hours before serving.

NUTRITION

- Calories: 341
- Fat: 34g
- Carbohydrates: 5g

PREPARATION: 30 MIN **COOKING: 90 MIN** **SERVES: 12**

172. SWEET ALMOND BITES

INGREDIENTS

- 18 ounces butter, grass-fed
- 2 ounces heavy cream
- ½ cup stevia
- 2/3 cup cocoa powder
- 1 teaspoon vanilla extract, pure
- 4 tablespoons almond butter

DIRECTIONS

1. Use a double boiler to melt your butter before adding all of your remaining ingredients.
2. Place the mixture into molds, freezing for two hours before serving.

NUTRITION

- Calories: 350
- Protein: 2g
- Fat: 38g

PREPARATION: 30 MIN **COOKING: 120 MIN** **SERVES: 12**

173. STRAWBERRY CHEESECAKE MINIS

INGREDIENTS

- 1 cup coconut oil
- 1 cup coconut butter
- ½ cup strawberries, sliced
- ½ teaspoon lime juice
- 2 tablespoons cream cheese, full fat
- Stevia to taste

DIRECTIONS

1. Blend your strawberries together.
2. Soften your cream cheese, and then add in your coconut butter.
3. Combine all the ingredients together, and then pour your mixture into silicone molds.
4. Freeze for at least two hours before serving.

NUTRITION

- Calories: 372
- Protein: 1g
- Fat: 41g
- Carbohydrates: 2g

 **PREPARATION: 10 MIN**
 **COOKING: 30 MIN**
 **SERVES: 12**

174. COCOA BROWNIES

INGREDIENTS

- 1 egg
- 2 tablespoons butter, grass-fed
- 2 teaspoons vanilla extract, pure
- ¼ teaspoon baking powder
- ¼ cup cocoa powder
- 1/3 cup heavy cream
- ¾ cup almond butter
- Pinch sea salt

DIRECTIONS

1. Break your egg into a bowl, whisking until smooth.
2. Add all of your wet ingredients, mixing well.
3. Mix all dry ingredients into a bowl.
4. Sift your dry ingredients into your wet ingredients, mixing to form a batter.
5. Get out a baking pan, greasing it before pouring in your mixture.
6. Heat your oven to 350°F and bake for twenty-five minutes.
7. Allow it to cool before slicing and serve room temperature or warm.

NUTRITION

- Calories: 184
- Protein: 1g
- Fat: 20g
- Carbohydrates: 1g

PREPARATION: 20 MIN **COOKING: 120 MIN** **SERVES: 6**

175. CHOCOLATE ORANGE BITES

INGREDIENTS

- 10 ounces coconut oil
- 4 tablespoons cocoa powder
- ¼ teaspoon blood orange extract
- Stevia to taste

DIRECTIONS

1. Melt half of your coconut oil using a double boiler, and then add in your stevia and orange extract.
2. Get out candy molds, pouring the mixture into it. Fill each mold halfway, and then place in the fridge until they set.
3. Melt the other half of your coconut oil, stirring in your cocoa powder and stevia, making sure that the mixture is smooth with no lumps.
4. Pour into your molds, filling them up all the way, and then allow it to set in the fridge before serving.

NUTRITION

- Calories: 188
- Protein: 1g
- Fat: 21g
- Carbohydrates: 5g

 **PREPARATION: 5 MIN**

 **COOKING: 25 MIN**

 SERVES: 2

176. ROASTED CAULIFLOWER WITH PROSCIUTTO, CAPERS, AND ALMONDS

INGREDIENTS

- 12 ounces cauliflower florets (I get precut florets at Trader Joe's)
- 2 tablespoons leftover bacon grease, or olive oil
- Pink Himalayan salt
- Freshly ground black pepper
- 2 ounces sliced prosciutto, torn into small pieces
- ¼ cup slivered almonds
- 2 tablespoons capers
- 2 tablespoons grated Parmesan cheese

DIRECTIONS

1. Preheat the oven to 400°F. Line a baking pan with a silicone baking mat or parchment paper.
2. Put the cauliflower florets in the prepared baking pan with the bacon grease, and season with pink Himalayan salt and pepper. Or if you are using olive oil instead, drizzle the cauliflower with olive oil and season with pink Himalayan salt and pepper.
3. Roast the cauliflower for 15 minutes.
4. Stir the cauliflower so all sides are coated with the bacon grease.
5. Distribute the prosciutto pieces in the pan. Then add the slivered almonds and capers. Stir to combine. Sprinkle the Parmesan cheese on top, and roast for 10 minutes more.
6. Divide between two plates, using a slotted spoon so you don't get excess grease in the plates, and serve.

NUTRITION

- Calories: 288
- Total Fat: 24g
- Carbs: 7g
- Net Carbs: 4g
- Fiber: 3g
- Protein: 14g

PREPARATION: 10 MIN   **COOKING: 4 HOURS**   **SERVES: 2**

177. BUTTERY SLOW-COOKER MUSHROOMS

INGREDIENTS

- 6 tablespoons butter
- 1 tablespoon packaged dry ranch-dressing mix
- 8 ounces fresh cremini mushrooms
- 2 tablespoons grated Parmesan cheese
- 1 tablespoon chopped fresh flat-leaf Italian parsley

DIRECTIONS

1. With the crock insert in place, preheat the slow cooker to low.
2. Put the butter and the dry ranch dressing in the bottom of the slow cooker, and allow the butter to melt. Stir to blend the dressing mix and butter.
3. Add the mushrooms to the slow cooker, and stir to coat with the butter-dressing mixture. Sprinkle the top with Parmesan cheese.
4. Cover and cook on low for 4 hours.
5. Use a slotted spoon to transfer the mushrooms to a serving dish. Top with the chopped parsley and serve.

NUTRITION

- Calories: 351
- Total Fat: 36g
- Carbs: 5g
- Net Carbs: 4g
- Fiber: 1g
- Protein: 6g

 **PREPARATION: 10 MIN**

 **COOKING: 25 MIN**

 **SERVES: 2**

178. BAKED ZUCCHINI GRATIN

INGREDIENTS

- 1 large zucchini, cut into ¼-inch-thick slices
- Pink Himalayan salt
- 1 ounce Brie cheese, rind trimmed off
- 1 tablespoon butter
- Freshly ground black pepper
- 1/3 cup shredded Gruyere cheese
- ¼ cup crushed pork rinds

DIRECTIONS

1. Salt the zucchini slices and put them in a colander in the sink for 45 minutes; the zucchini will shed much of their water.
2. Preheat the oven to 400°F.
3. When the zucchini has been "weeping" for about 30 minutes, in a small saucepan over medium-low heat, heat the Brie and butter, stirring occasionally, until the cheese has melted and the mixture is fully combined, about 2 minutes.
4. Arrange the zucchini in an 8-inch baking dish so the zucchini slices are overlapping a bit. Season with pepper.
5. Pour the Brie mixture over the zucchini, and top with the shredded Gruyere cheese.
6. Sprinkle the crushed pork rinds over the top.
7. Bake for about 25 minutes, until the dish is bubbling and the top is nicely browned, and serve.

NUTRITION

- Calories: 355
- Total Fat: 25g
- Carbs: 5g
- Net Carbs: 4g
- Fiber: 2g
- Protein: 28g

PREPARATION: 10 MIN **COOKING: 15 MIN** **SERVES: 2**

179. ROASTED RADISHES WITH BROWN BUTTER SAUCE

INGREDIENTS

- 2 cups halved radishes
- 1 tablespoon olive oil
- Pink Himalayan salt
- Freshly ground black pepper
- 2 tablespoons butter
- 1 tablespoon chopped fresh flat-leaf Italian parsley

DIRECTIONS

1. Preheat the oven to 450°F.
2. In a medium bowl, toss the radishes in olive oil and season with pink Himalayan salt and pepper.
3. Spread the radishes on a baking sheet in a single layer. Roast for 15 minutes, stirring halfway through.
4. Meanwhile, when the radishes have been roasting for about 10 minutes, in a small, light-colored saucepan over medium heat, melt the butter completely, stirring frequently, and season with pink Himalayan salt. When the butter begins to bubble and foam, continue stirring. When the bubbling diminishes a bit, the butter should be a nice nutty brown. The browning process should take about 3 minutes total. Transfer the browned butter to a heat-safe container (I use a mug).
5. Remove the radishes from the oven, and divide them between two plates. Spoon the brown butter over the radishes, top with the chopped parsley, and serve.

NUTRITION

- Calories: 181
- Total Fat: 19g
- Carbs: 4g
- Net Carbs: 2g
- Fiber: 2g
- Protein: 1g

PREPARATION: 5 MIN **COOKING: 15 MIN** **SERVES: 2**

180. PARMESAN AND PORK RIND GREEN BEANS

INGREDIENTS

- ½ pound fresh green beans
- 2 tablespoons crushed pork rinds
- 2 tablespoons olive oil
- 1 tablespoon grated Parmesan cheese
- Pink Himalayan salt
- Freshly ground black pepper

DIRECTIONS

1. Preheat the oven to 400°F.
2. In a medium bowl, combine the green beans, pork rinds, olive oil, and Parmesan cheese. Season with pink Himalayan salt and pepper, and toss until the beans are thoroughly coated.
3. Spread the bean mixture on a baking sheet in a single layer, and roast for about 15 minutes. At the halfway point, give the pan a little shake to move the beans around, or just give them a stir.
4. Divide the beans between two plates and serve.

NUTRITION

- Calories: 175
- Total Fat: 15g
- Carbs: 8g
- Net Carbs: 5g
- Fiber: 3g
- Protein: 6g

PREPARATION: 5 MIN

COOKING: 20 MIN

SERVES: 2

181. PESTO CAULIFLOWER STEAKS

INGREDIENTS

- 2 tablespoons olive oil, plus more for brushing
- ½ head cauliflower
- Pink Himalayan salt
- Freshly ground black pepper
- 2 cups fresh basil leaves
- ½ cup grated Parmesan cheese
- ¼ cup almonds
- ½ cup shredded mozzarella cheese

DIRECTIONS

1. Preheat the oven to 425°F. Brush a baking sheet with olive oil or line with a silicone baking mat.
2. To prep, the cauliflower steaks, remove and discard the leaves and cut the cauliflower into 1-inch-thick slices. You can roast the extra floret crumbles that fall off with the steaks.
3. Place the cauliflower steaks on the prepared baking sheet, and brush them with olive oil. You want the surface just lightly coated so it gets caramelized. Season with pink Himalayan salt and pepper.
4. Roast the cauliflower steaks for 20 minutes.
5. Meanwhile, put the basil, Parmesan cheese, almonds, and 2 tablespoons of olive oil in a food processor (or blender), and season with pink Himalayan salt and pepper. Mix until combined.
6. Spread some pesto on top of each cauliflower steak, and top with the mozzarella cheese. Return to the oven and bake until the cheese melts, about 2 minutes.
7. Place the cauliflower steaks on two plates, and serve hot.

NUTRITION

- Calories: 448
- Total Fat: 34g
- Carbs: 17g
- Net Carbs: 10g
- Fiber: 7g
- Protein: 24g

PREPARATION: 30 MIN   **COOKING: 0 MIN**   **SERVES: 2**

182. TOMATO, AVOCADO, AND CUCUMBER SALAD

INGREDIENTS

- ½ cup grape tomatoes, halved
- 4 small Persian cucumbers or 1 English cucumber, peeled and finely chopped
- 1 avocado, finely chopped
- ¼ cup crumbled feta cheese
- 2 tablespoons vinaigrette salad dressing (I use Primal Kitchen Greek Vinaigrette)
- Pink Himalayan salt
- Freshly ground black pepper

DIRECTIONS

1. In a large bowl, combine the tomatoes, cucumbers, avocado, and feta cheese.
2. Add the vinaigrette, and season with pink Himalayan salt and pepper. Toss to thoroughly combine.
3. Divide the salad between two plates and serve.

NUTRITION

- Calories: 258
- Total Fat: 23g
- Carbs: 12g
- Net Carbs: 6g
- Fiber: 6g
- Protein: 5g

PREPARATION: 5 MIN

COOKING: 25 MIN

SERVES: 2

183. CRUNCHY PORK RIND ZUCCHINI STICKS

INGREDIENTS

- 2 medium zucchinis, halved lengthwise and seeded
- ¼ cup crushed pork rinds
- ¼ cup grated Parmesan cheese
- 2 garlic cloves, minced
- 2 tablespoons melted butter
- Pink Himalayan salt
- Freshly ground black pepper
- Olive oil, for drizzling

DIRECTIONS

1. Preheat the oven to 400°F. Line a baking sheet with aluminum foil or a silicone baking mat.
2. Place the zucchini halves cut-side up on the prepared baking sheet.
3. In a medium bowl, combine the pork rinds, Parmesan cheese, garlic, and melted butter, and season with pink Himalayan salt and pepper. Mix until well combined.
4. Spoon the pork-rind mixture onto each zucchini stick, and drizzle each with a little olive oil.
5. Bake for about 20 minutes, or until the topping is golden brown.
6. Turn on the broiler to finish browning the zucchini sticks, 3 to 5 minutes, and serve.

NUTRITION

- Calories: 231
- Total Fat: 20g
- Carbs: 8g
- Fiber: 2g
- Protein: 9g

PREPARATION: 10 MIN **COOKING: 10 MIN** **SERVES: 2**

184. CHEESE CHIPS AND GUACAMOLE

INGREDIENTS

For the cheese chips
- 1 cup shredded cheese (I use Mexican blend)

For the guacamole
- 1 avocado, mashed
- Juice of ½ lime
- 1 teaspoon diced jalapeño
- 2 tablespoons chopped fresh cilantro leaves
- Pink Himalayan salt
- Freshly ground black pepper

DIRECTIONS

1. Preheat the oven to 350°F. Line a baking sheet with parchment paper or a silicone baking mat.
2. Add ¼-cup mounds of shredded cheese to the pan, leaving plenty of space between them, and bake until the edges are brown and the middles have fully melted, about 7 minutes.
3. Set the pan on a cooling rack, and let the cheese chips cool for 5 minutes. The chips will be floppy when they first come out of the oven but will crisp as they cool.
4. In a medium bowl, mix together the avocado, lime juice, jalapeño, and cilantro, and season with pink Himalayan salt and pepper.
5. Top the cheese chips with the guacamole, and serve.

NUTRITION

- Calories: 323;
- Total Fat: 27g;
- Carbs: 8g;
- Net Carbs: 3g;
- Fiber: 5g
- Protein: 15g

PREPARATION: 10 MIN

COOKING: 25 MIN

SERVES: 2

185. CAULIFLOWER "POTATO" SALAD

INGREDIENTS

- ½ head cauliflower
- 1 tablespoon olive oil
- Pink Himalayan salt
- Freshly ground black pepper
- 1/3 cup mayonnaise
- 1 tablespoon mustard
- ¼ cup diced dill pickles
- 1 teaspoon paprika

DIRECTIONS

1. Preheat the oven to 400°F. Line a baking sheet with aluminum foil or a silicone baking mat.
2. Cut the cauliflower into 1-inch pieces.
3. Put the cauliflower in a large bowl, add the olive oil, season with the pink Himalayan salt and pepper, and toss to combine.
4. Spread the cauliflower out on the prepared baking sheet and bake for 25 minutes, or just until the cauliflower begins to brown. Halfway through the cooking time, give the pan a couple of shakes or stir so all sides of the cauliflower cook.
5. In a large bowl, mix the cauliflower together with the mayonnaise, mustard, and pickles. Sprinkle the paprika on top, and chill in the refrigerator for 3 hours before serving.

NUTRITION

- Calories: 386
- Total Fat: 37g
- Carbs: 13g
- Net Carbs: 8g
- Fiber: 5g
- Protein: 5g

PREPARATION: 10 MIN

COOKING: 10 MIN

SERVES: 4

186. LOADED CAULIFLOWER MASHED "POTATOES"

INGREDIENTS

- 1 head fresh cauliflower, cut into cubes
- 2 garlic cloves, minced
- 6 tablespoons butter
- 2 tablespoons sour cream
- Pink Himalayan salt
- Freshly ground black pepper
- 1 cup shredded cheese (I use Colby Jack)
- 6 bacon slices, cooked and crumbled

DIRECTIONS

1. Boil a large pot of water over high heat. Add the cauliflower. Reduce the heat to medium-low and simmer for 8 to 10 minutes, until fork-tender. (You can also steam the cauliflower if you have a steamer basket.)
2. Drain the cauliflower in a colander, and turn it out onto a paper towel-lined plate to soak up the water. Blot to remove any remaining water from the cauliflower pieces. This step is important; you want to get out as much water as possible so the mash won't be runny.
3. Add the cauliflower to the food processor (or blender) with the garlic, butter, and sour cream, and season with pink Himalayan salt and pepper.
4. Mix for about 1 minute, stopping to scrape down the sides of the bowl every 30 seconds.
5. Divide the cauliflower mix evenly among four small serving dishes, and top each with the cheese and bacon crumbles. (The cheese should melt from the hot cauliflower. But if you want to reheat it, you can put the cauliflower in oven-safe serving dishes and pop them under the broiler for 1 minute to heat up the cauliflower and melt the cheese.)
6. Serve warm.

NUTRITION

- Calories: 757
- Total Fat: 38g
- Carbs: 17g
- Net Carbs: 11g
- Fiber: 6g
- Protein: 29g

PREPARATION: 5 MIN   **COOKING: 25 MIN**   **SERVES: 6**

187. KETO BREAD

INGREDIENTS

- 5 tablespoons butter, at room temperature, divided
- 6 large eggs, lightly beaten
- 1½ cups almond flour
- 3 teaspoons baking powder
- 1 scoop MCT oil powder
- Pinch pink Himalayan salt

DIRECTIONS

1. Preheat the oven to 390°F. Coat a 9-by-5-inch loaf pan with 1 tablespoon of butter.
2. In a large bowl, use a hand mixer to mix the eggs, almond flour, remaining 4 tablespoons of butter, baking powder, MCT oil powder (if using), and pink Himalayan salt until thoroughly blended. Pour into the prepared pan.
3. Bake for 25 minutes, or until a toothpick inserted in the center comes out clean.
4. Slice and serve.

NUTRITION

- Calories: 165
- Total Fat: 15g
- Carbs: 4g
- Net Carbs: 2g
- Fiber: 2g
- Protein: 6g

PREPARATION: 30 MIN

COOKING: 15 MIN

SERVES: 8

188. DEVILED EGGS

INGREDIENTS

- 12 large eggs
- ½ cup mayonnaise
- ¼ cup sour cream
- 1 tablespoon ground mustard
- Pink Himalayan salt
- Freshly ground black pepper
- 1 teaspoon paprika

DIRECTIONS

1. To hard-boil the eggs, place the eggs in a large saucepan and cover with 3 to 4 inches of water. Bring the water to a boil, turn off the heat, cover the pot, and let sit for 15 minutes. Drain the eggs and fill the pan with ice-cold water (you can add ice cubes, too). One by one, lightly tap the eggs on the countertop to crack and then peel them under cold running water. Put them on a paper towel-lined plate.
2. Halve the eggs lengthwise. With a small spoon, carefully remove the yolks, transfer the yolks to a small bowl, and mash them.
3. Add the mayonnaise, sour cream, and mustard, and season with pink Himalayan salt and pepper. Mix with a fork until smooth.
4. Spoon the yolk mixture back into the indentations in the egg whites, or pipe it in with a cake-decorating bag if you want it to look pretty. Sprinkle with the paprika and serve.

NUTRITION

- Calories: 74
- Total Fat: 7g
- Carbs: 1g
- Net Carbs: 0g
- Fiber: 0g
- Protein: 3g

PREPARATION: 15 MIN **COOKING: 0 MIN** **SERVES: 2**

189. CHICKEN-PECAN SALAD CUCUMBER BITES

INGREDIENTS

- 1 cup diced cooked chicken breast
- 2 tablespoons mayonnaise
- ¼ cup chopped pecans
- ¼ cup diced celery
- Pink Himalayan salt
- Freshly ground black pepper
- 1 cucumber, peeled and cut into ¼-inch slices

DIRECTIONS

1. In a medium bowl, mix together the chicken, mayonnaise, pecans, and celery. Season with pink Himalayan salt and pepper.
2. Lay the cucumber slices out on a plate, and add a pinch of pink Himalayan salt to each.
3. Top each cucumber slice with a spoonful of the chicken-salad mixture and serve.

NUTRITION

- Calories: 323
- Total Fat: 24g
- Carbs: 6g
- Net Carbs: 4g
- Fiber: 3g
- Protein: 23g

PREPARATION: 10 MIN

COOKING: 20 MIN

SERVES: 2

190. BUFFALO CHICKEN DIP

INGREDIENTS

- Butter or olive oil, for greasing the pan
- 1 large cooked boneless chicken breast, shredded
- 8 ounces cream cheese
- ½ cup shredded Cheddar cheese
- ½ cup chunky blue cheese dressing
- ¼ cup buffalo wing sauce

DIRECTIONS

1. Preheat the oven to 375°F. Grease a small baking pan.
2. In a medium bowl, mix together the chicken, cream cheese, Cheddar cheese, blue cheese dressing, and wing sauce. Transfer the mixture to the prepared baking pan.
3. Bake for 20 minutes.
4. Pour into a dip dish and serve hot.

NUTRITION

- Calories: 859
- Total Fat: 73g
- Carbs: 8g
- Net Carbs: 8g
- Fiber: 0g
- Protein: 41g

PREPARATION: 5 MIN **COOKING: 25 MIN** **SERVES: 2**

191. ROASTED BRUSSELS SPROUTS WITH BACON

INGREDIENTS

- ½ pound Brussels sprouts, cleaned, trimmed, and halved
- 1 tablespoon olive oil
- Pink Himalayan salt
- Freshly ground black pepper
- 1 teaspoon red pepper flakes
- 6 bacon slices
- 1 tablespoon grated Parmesan cheese

DIRECTIONS

1. Preheat the oven to 400°F.
2. In a medium bowl, toss the Brussels sprouts with the olive oil, season with pink Himalayan salt and pepper, and add the red pepper flakes.
3. Cut the bacon strips into 1-inch pieces. (I use kitchen shears.)
4. Place the Brussels sprouts and bacon on a baking sheet in a single layer. Roast for about 25 minutes. About halfway through the baking time, give the pan a little shake to move the sprouts around, or give them a stir. You want your Brussels sprouts crispy and browned on the outside.
5. Remove the Brussels sprouts from the oven. Divide them between two plates, top each serving with Parmesan cheese, and serve.

NUTRITION

- Calories: 248
- Total Fat: 18g
- Carbs: 11g
- Net Carbs: 7g
- Fiber: 5g
- Protein: 14g

PREPARATION: 20 MIN **COOKING: 0 MIN** **SERVES: 2**

192. SALAMI, PEPPERONCINI, AND CREAM CHEESE PINWHEELS

INGREDIENTS

- 8 ounces cream cheese, at room temperature
- ¼ pound salami, thinly sliced
- 2 tablespoons sliced pepperoncini

DIRECTIONS

1. Lay out a sheet of plastic wrap on a large cutting board or counter.
2. Place the cream cheese in the center of the plastic wrap, and then add another layer of plastic wrap on top. Using a rolling pin, roll the cream cheese until it is even and about ¼ inch thick. Try to make the shape somewhat resemble a rectangle.
3. Pull off the top layer of plastic wrap.
4. Place the salami slices so they overlap to completely cover the cream-cheese layer.
5. Place a new piece of plastic wrap on top of the salami layer so that you can flip over your cream cheese–salami rectangle. Flip the layer so the cream cheese side is up.
6. Remove the plastic wrap and add the sliced pepperoncini in a layer on top.
7. Roll the layered ingredients into a tight log, pressing the meat and cream cheese together. (You want it as tight as possible.) Then wrap the roll with plastic wrap and refrigerate for at least 6 hours so it will set.
8. Use a sharp knife to cut the log into slices and serve.

NUTRITION

- Calories: 583
- Total Fat: 54g
- Carbs: 7g
- Net Carbs: 7g
- Fiber: 0g
- Protein: 19g

PREPARATION: 5 MIN **COOKING: 20 MIN** **SERVES: 2**

193. CAULIFLOWER STEAKS WITH BACON AND BLUE CHEESE

INGREDIENTS

- ½ head cauliflower
- 1 tablespoon olive oil
- Pink Himalayan salt
- Freshly ground black pepper
- 4 bacon slices
- 2 tablespoons blue cheese salad dressing

DIRECTIONS

1. Preheat the oven to 425°F. Line a baking sheet with aluminum foil or a silicone baking mat.
2. To prep the cauliflower steaks, remove and discard the leaves and cut the cauliflower into 1-inch-thick slices. You can also roast the extra floret crumbles that fall off with the steaks.
3. Place the cauliflower steaks on the prepared baking sheet, and brush with the olive oil. You want the surface just lightly coated with the oil so it gets caramelized. Season with pink Himalayan salt and pepper. Place the bacon slices on the pan, along with the cauliflower floret crumbles.
4. Roast the cauliflower steaks for 20 minutes.
5. Place the cauliflower steaks on two plates. Drizzle with blue cheese dressing, top with crumbled bacon, and serve.

NUTRITION

- Calories: 254
- Total Fat: 19g
- Carbs: 11g
- Net Carbs: 7g
- Fiber: 4g
- Protein: 11g

PREPARATION: 10 MIN

COOKING: 20 MIN

SERVES: 4

194. BACON-WRAPPED JALAPEÑOS

INGREDIENTS

- 10 jalapeños
- 8 ounces cream cheese, at room temperature
- 1 pound bacon

DIRECTIONS

1. Preheat the oven to 450°F. Line a baking sheet with aluminum foil or a silicone baking mat.
2. Halve the jalapeños lengthwise, and remove the seeds and membranes (if you like the extra heat, leave them in). Place them on the prepared pan cut-side up.
3. Spread some of the cream cheese inside each jalapeño half.
4. Wrap a jalapeño half with a slice of bacon (depending on the size of the jalapeño, use a whole slice of bacon, or half).
5. Secure the bacon around each jalapeño with 1 to 2 toothpicks so it stays put while baking.
6. Bake for 20 minutes, until the bacon is done and crispy.
7. Serve hot or at room temperature. Either way, they are delicious!

NUTRITION

- Calories: 164
- Total Fat: 13g
- Carbs: 1g
- Net Carbs: 1g
- Fiber: 0g
- Protein: 9g

PREPARATION: 10 MIN

COOKING: 10 MIN

SERVES: 2

195. CREAMY BROCCOLI-BACON SALAD

INGREDIENTS

- 6 bacon slices
- ½ pound fresh broccoli, cut into small florets
- ¼ cup sliced almonds
- 1/3 cup mayonnaise
- 1 tablespoon honey mustard dressing

DIRECTIONS

1. In a large skillet over medium-high heat, cook the bacon on both sides until crispy, about 8 minutes. Transfer the bacon to a paper towel–lined plate to drain and cool for 5 minutes. When cool, break the bacon into crumbles.
2. In a large bowl, combine the broccoli with the almonds and bacon.
3. In a small bowl, mix together the mayonnaise and honey mustard.
4. Add the dressing to the broccoli salad, and toss to thoroughly combine.
5. Chill the salad for 1 hour or more before serving.

NUTRITION

- Calories: 549
- Total Fat: 49g
- Carbs: 16g
- Net Carbs: 11g
- Fiber: 5g
- Protein: 16g

14. DESSERTS RECIPES

PREPARATION: 15 MIN

COOKING: 40 MIN

SERVES: 8

196. SOUTHERN APPLE PIE

INGREDIENTS

Crust:
- 2 cups blanched almond flour
- ½ cup butter
- ½ cup powdered Erythritol
- 1 teaspoon allspice

Filling:
- 3 cups sliced apples
- ¼ cup melted butter
- ½ lemon, juiced
- ¼ cup powdered Erythritol
- ½ teaspoon allspice

Topping:
- Cinnamon, as desired
- Granulated Erythritol, as desired

DIRECTIONS

1. Prepare the crust; preheat oven to 375°F.
2. Melt the butter in a microwave-safe bowl.
3. Combine almond flour, melted butter, and the remaining crust ingredients until the dough comes together.
4. Press the crust into the 9-inch springform.
5. Cover the crust with parchment paper and baking balls (or rice) and bake 10 minutes.
6. In the meantime, make the filling; toss the sliced apples with juice.
7. Remove the crust from the oven. Fill with the apples in a circular pattern.
8. Combine butter, Erythritol, and allspice in a bowl.
9. Pour over the apples.
10. Bake the pie for 30 minutes.
11. Remove the pie from the oven and allow to cool.
12. Combine desired amounts of cinnamon and Erythritol.
13. Sprinkle the apples with the cinnamon mixture.
14. Slice and serve.

NUTRITION

- Calories: 123
- Fat: 9.2g
- Carbs: 4.8g
- Protein: 8.3g

PREPARATION: 15 MIN   **COOKING: 25 MIN**   **SERVES: 8**

197. CHEESE BERRY PIE

INGREDIENTS

Crust:
- 1 cup coconut oil, solid
- 4 large eggs
- 1 pinch salt
- 1 ½ cups softened coconut flour
- 1 tablespoon cold water
- ½ teaspoon baking powder

Filling:
- 1(½) cups fresh blueberries
- 2 tablespoons granulated Erythritol
- 1 cup cream cheese

DIRECTIONS

1. Preheat oven to 350°F.
2. Make the crust; combine coconut flour, salt, and baking powder in a bowl.
3. Work in coconut oil.
4. Add eggs, one at the time until incorporated.
5. Add water and stir until you have a smooth dough. Divide the dough into two equal parts.
6. Transfer the one part into 9-inch pie pan. Roll out the second and place aside.
7. Prepare the filling; spread cream cheese over the crust.
8. Toss the blueberries with the Erythritol and spread over the cheese.
9. Top the pie with the remaining dough.
10. Bake the pie for 25 minutes.
11. Cool the pie on a rack for 10 minutes.
12. Slice and serve.

NUTRITION

- Calories: 143
- Fat: 9.2g
- Carbs: 4.8g
- Protein: 8.3g

PREPARATION: 15 MIN **COOKING: 25 MIN** **SERVES: 12**

198. LEMON CHEESECAKE

INGREDIENTS

Crust:
- 2 teaspoons granulated Erythritol
- 2 cups almond flour
- ½ cup unsalted melted butter
- ¼ cup desiccated coconut

Filling:
- 1 tablespoon powdered gelatin
- 2 tablespoons granulated Erythritol
- ¾ cup boiling water
- ½ cup cold water
- 1 pound cream cheese
- 2 lemons, zested and juiced

DIRECTIONS

1. Prepare the crust; combine the crust ingredients in a large mixing bowl.
2. Stir until the dough comes together.
3. Transfer the dough into 9-inch springform.
4. Place in a fridge while you make the filling.
5. Prepare the filling; pour the water in a bowl. Sprinkle over the gelatin powder. Pour in cold water and place aside for 5 minutes.
6. Beat cream cheese, gelatin mixture, Erythritol, lemon juice and zest in a mixing bowl.
7. Pour the filling over the crust.
8. Refrigerate for 2 hours.
9. Slice and serve.

NUTRITION

- Calories: 143
- Fat: 9.2g
- Carbs: 4.8g
- Protein: 8.3g

PREPARATION: 15 MINUTES + INACTIVE TIME.

COOKING: 25 MIN

SERVES: 8

199. NO-GUILT CHOCOLATE CAKE

INGREDIENTS

- ¾ cup butter
- 12 ounces sugar-free quality dark chocolate, chopped or chocolate chips
- 1 teaspoon sugar-free vanilla extract
- 3 large eggs, room temperature
- 1 pinch salt
- ¼ cup granulated Erythritol
- 10 drops liquid Stevia

DIRECTIONS

1. Preheat oven to 350°F.
2. Line 8-inch springform pan with baking paper. Additionally, grease with some coconut oil for easy removal.
3. Melt butter and chopped chocolate over a double boiler.
4. Remove from the heat and pour the mixture into a large bowl.
5. Beat in vanilla and salt.
6. Beat in the eggs, one at the time, and beating well after each addition.
7. Fold in the sweetener.
8. Strain the mixture through a fine sieve into the prepared springform.
9. Gently tap the springform onto the kitchen counter.
10. Bake the cake for 25 minutes.
11. Cool the cake to room temperature and refrigerate for at least 8 hours.
12. Slice and serve, with a dollop of whipped coconut cream.

NUTRITION

- Calories: 103
- Fat: 9.2g
- Carbs: 4.8g
- Protein: 8.3g

PREPARATION: 15 MIN

COOKING: 10 MIN

SERVES: 16

200. THE BEST COOKIES

INGREDIENTS

- 1/3 cup coconut oil
- 1(½) teaspoon sugar-free vanilla extract
- 1 medium egg
- 1 pinch of salt
- 3 tablespoons granulated Erythritol
- 1 cup almond flour
- 2 tablespoons coconut flour
- ½ teaspoon cinnamon
- 1/3 cup sugar-free quality dark chocolate chips

DIRECTIONS

1. Preheat oven to 350°F. Line baking sheet with a parchment paper.
2. In a mixing bowl, beat egg with vanilla and Erythritol.
3. Melt the coconut oil and fold into the egg mixture.
4. Fold the remaining ingredients and stir until the dough comes together.
5. Let the dough stand for 5 minutes.
6. Scoop the dough with a cookie scoop, onto the baking sheet.
7. Press gently with the back of your spoon to flatten.
8. Bake the cookies for 10 minutes.
9. Cool briefly on a wire rack before serving.
10. Serve with a cup of almond milk and enjoy.

NUTRITION

- Calories: 143,
- Fat: 9.2g
- Carbs 4.8g
- Protein: 8.3g

PREPARATION: 15 MIN **COOKING: 25 MIN** **SERVES: 10**

201. SALTY CARAMEL CAKE

INGREDIENTS

- 2 cups blanched almond flour
- 3 tablespoons coconut flour
- 2 tablespoons vanilla whey protein powder
- ¾ tablespoon baking powder
- 1/3 cup unsalted butter
- 1 pinch salt
- ½ cup granulated Erythritol
- 3 large eggs, room temperature
- 1 teaspoon sugar-free vanilla extract
- ½ cup unsweetened almond milk
- 2 cups sugar-free caramel sauce
- Sea salt flakes, for sprinkle

DIRECTIONS

1. Preheat oven to 325°F.
2. Line 2(8-inch) springform pans with baking paper.
3. In a mixing bowl, combine all the dry ingredients, except the sweetener.
4. In a separate bowl, cream butter, and Erythritol.
5. Beat in eggs, one at the time, followed by vanilla and almond milk.
6. Fold the liquid ingredients into the dry ones.
7. Divide the batter between two springform pans.
8. Bake the sponges for 25 minutes or until the inserted toothpick comes out clean.
9. Place the sponges and aside to cool.
10. Spread 1(½) cups of the caramel sauce over one sponge. Top with the second sponge.
11. Pour the remaining caramel over the top.
12. Sprinkle the caramel with salt flakes. Refrigerate the cake for 1 hour. Slice and serve.

NUTRITION

- Calories: 143
- Fat: 9.2g
- Carbs: 4.8g
- Protein: 8.3g

PREPARATION: 15 MINUTES + INACTIVE TIME. **COOKING: 25 MIN** **SERVES: 10**

202. LUSCIOUS RED VELVET CAKE

INGREDIENTS

Cake:
- 1 cup granulated Erythritol
- ½ cup coconut flour
- ½ cup Swerve
- 2 tablespoons raw cocoa powder
- 6 large eggs, separated
- ½ cup melted and cooled butter
- 2 tablespoons crème Fraiche
- 1 tablespoon powdered red food coloring
- 1 teaspoon white vinegar
- 1 teaspoon sugar-free vanilla

Frosting:
- 4 ounces cream cheese
- 4 tablespoons softened unsalted butter
- 2 cups Swerve
- 1 tablespoon heavy cream
- ½ teaspoon sugar-free vanilla extract

DIRECTIONS

1. Preheat oven to 350°F.
2. Line 9-inch springform with a baking paper and grease with some coconut oil.
3. Combine all the dry ingredients in a large mixing bowl.
4. In a separate bowl, beat eggs, butter, crème Fraiche, vinegar, and vanilla.
5. Fold the liquid ingredients into the dry ones and stir until smooth.
6. Pour the batter into the springform.
7. Bake the cake for 25–30 minutes or until the inserted toothpick comes out clean.
8. Make the frosting; beat cream cheese and butter in a bowl until fluffy.
9. Add sugar and heavy cream.
10. Beat until smooth.
11. Remove the cake from the springform once completely cold.
12. Top with the frosting.
13. Refrigerate the cake for 30 minutes.
14. Slice and serve.

NUTRITION

- Calories: 143
- Fat: 9.2g
- Carbs: 4.8g
- Protein: 8.3g

PREPARATION: 15 MIN

COOKING: 50 MIN

SERVES: 10

203. SOUTHERN PECAN PIE

INGREDIENTS

Crust:
- 3 cups blanched almond flour
- 4 large eggs, room temperature
- ½ cup unsalted melted butter
- ½ cup Swerve
1 good pinch salt
- **Filling:**
- 1 cup coconut oil or butter
- ¾ cup golden Swerve
- ½ cup granulated Erythritol
- 1(½) tablespoon sugar-free maple syrup
- 4 large eggs, room temperature
- 1(½) cup pecans, chopped
- ¾ cup pecan halves
- 2 teaspoon vanilla-bourbon extract

DIRECTIONS

1. Preheat oven to 325°F.
2. Grease 10-inch cast-iron skillet with butter.
3. In a large mixing bowl, combine the crust ingredients until the smooth dough is formed.
4. Transfer the dough into the skillet and press, so you cover the bottom and sides.
5. Prepare the filling; melt butter in a saucepot and fold in sweeteners and sugar-free maple syrup. Stir until the sweeteners are dissolved. Place aside to cool.
6. Beat the eggs with cold syrup until fluffy. Fold in pecan pieces.
7. Pour the sauce into the crust.
8. Top with pecan halves.
9. Cover the pie with an aluminum foil. Bake the pie for 40 minutes.
10. Cool before slicing and serving.

NUTRITION

- Calories: 143
- Fat: 9.2g
- Carbs: 4.8g
- Protein: 8.3g

PREPARATION: 5 MIN

COOKING: 35 MIN

SERVES: 8

204. CHIA SEED CRACKERS

INGREDIENTS

- 1/2 cup ground chia seeds
- 1 1/2 cups water
- 1/4 teaspoon paprika
- 1/4 teaspoon black pepper
- 1/4 teaspoon dried oregano
- 3 ounces shredded cheddar cheese
- 2 tablespoon almond meal
- 1/4 teaspoon garlic powder
- 4 tablespoon olive oil
- 1/4 teaspoon salt

DIRECTIONS

1. Preheat oven to 375°F and in the meantime take a large bowl and mix oregano, garlic powder, almond meal, paprika, chia seeds, salt and pepper. Mix together until all the ingredients are well combined.
2. Take the olive oil and pour into the mixture. Whisk until fully blended.
3. Pour water into the mixture and keep mixing until you see the smoothness.
4. Add the shredded cheddar cheese, mix it well with the mixture using a spatula and then prepare the dough kneading with your hands.
5. Spread the dough on a parchment paper in the baking sheet, cover with another parchment paper from the top and make it 0.125 inches thin with the help of a roller.
6. Place in the preheated oven and bake for 30 minutes.
7. Cut into the shapes you like after removing from the oven and place in the oven again to bake for 5 minutes more or until the time you are satisfied.
8. Remove from the oven once properly baked and transfer to the wire rack to cool before you serve the delicious chia seed crackers.

NUTRITION

- Calories: 120
- Fat: 13g
- Carbohydrates: 2g
- Protein: 4g

PREPARATION: 20 MIN

COOKING: 20 MIN

SERVES: 9

205. CHEESY BISCUITS

INGREDIENTS

- 4 eggs
- 2 cups almond flour
- 2 ½ cups shredded cheddar cheese
- 1/4 cup half-and-half
- 1 tablespoon baking powder

DIRECTIONS

1. Preheat oven to 350°F and get the baking sheet ready by lining it with parchment paper.
2. Take a large bowl and mix the baking powder and almond flour in that.
3. Add cheddar cheese to the mixture and mix until well combined.
4. Take a small bowl, add half and half and also crack the eggs into it. Mix well until fully blended.
5. Add the eggs mixture to the flour mixture and keep whisking with the help of a spatula to prepare a smooth batter.
6. Take portions of the batter using a scoop and put them on the baking sheet. Make sure that you take the portions in even sizes and flatten them a bit from the top.
7. Place in the preheated oven and bake for 20 minutes or until the time you get a golden-brown look.
8. Remove from the oven once baked and transfer to the wire rack to cool before serving.

NUTRITION

- Calories: 320
- Fat: 27g
- Carbohydrates: 8g
- Protein: 15g

PREPARATION: 15 MIN

COOKING: 0 MIN

SERVES: 2

206. KETO COCONUT FLAKE BALLS

INGREDIENTS

- 1 Vanilla shortbread collagen protein bar
- 1 tablespoon lemon
- ¼ teaspoon ground ginger
- ½ cup unsweetened coconut flakes,
- ¼ teaspoon ground turmeric

DIRECTIONS

1. Process protein bar, ginger, turmeric, and ¾ of the total flakes into a food processor.
2. Remove and add a spoon of water and roll till dough forms.
3. Roll into balls, and sprinkle the rest of the flakes on it. Serve.

NUTRITION

- Calories: 204
- Total Fat: 11g
- Total Carbs: 4.2g
- Protein: 1.5g

PREPARATION: 10 MIN   **COOKING: 15 MIN**   **SERVES: 4**

207. TOFU NUGGETS WITH CILANTRO DIP

INGREDIENTS

- 1 lime, ½ juiced, and ½ cut into wedges
- 1½ cups olive oil
- 28 oz tofu, pressed and cubed
- 1 egg, lightly beaten
- 1 cup golden flaxseed meal
- 1 ripe avocado, chopped
- ½ tablespoon chopped cilantro
- Salt and black pepper to taste
- ½ tablespoon olive oil

DIRECTIONS

1. Heat olive oil in a deep skillet. Coat tofu cubes in the egg and then in the flaxseed meal. Fry until golden brown. Transfer to a plate.
2. Place avocado, cilantro, salt, pepper, and lime juice in a blender; puree until smooth. Spoon into a bowl, add tofu nuggets, and lime wedges to serve.

NUTRITION

- Calories: 665
- Net Carbs: 6.2g
- Fat: 54g
- Protein: 32g

PREPARATION: 15 MIN	**COOKING: 30 MIN**	**SERVES: 3**

208. KETO CHOCOLATE GREEK YOGHURT COOKIES

INGREDIENTS

- 3 eggs
- 1/8 teaspoon tartar
- 5 tablespoons softened Greek yogurt

DIRECTIONS

1. Beat the egg whites, the tartar, and mix.
2. In the yolk, put in the Greek yogurt, and mix.
3. Combine both egg whites and yolk batter into a bowl.
4. Bake for 25–30 minutes, serve.

NUTRITION

- Calories: 287
- Total Fat: 19g
- Total Carbs: 6.5g
- Protein: 6.8g

PREPARATION: 20 MIN

COOKING: 1H 15 MIN

SERVES: 6

209. CHOCOLATE DIPPED CANDIED BACON

INGREDIENTS

- ½ teaspoon Cinnamon
- 2 tablespoon brown sugar alternative – ex. Surkin Gold
- 16 thin-cut slices of bacon
- ½ oz. cacao butter or coconut oil
- 3 oz. 85% dark chocolate
- 1 teaspoon Sugar-free maple extract

DIRECTIONS

1. Whisk the Surkin Gold and cinnamon together.
2. Arrange the bacon strips on a parchment paper-lined tray and sprinkle using half of the mixture. Do the other side with the rest of the seasoning mixture.
3. Set the oven to reach 275° Fahrenheit. Bake until caramelized and crispy (approximately 1 hour and 15 minutes).
4. Heat a skillet to melt the cocoa butter and chocolate. Pour the maple syrup into the mixture and stir well. Set aside until it's room temperature.
5. Arrange the bacon on a platter to cool thoroughly before dipping it into the chocolate.
6. Dip half of each strip of the bacon into the chocolate.
7. Arrange on a tray for the chocolate to solidify. Either place it in the refrigerator or on the countertop.

NUTRITION

- Calorie Count: 54
- Protein: 3 g
- Fat: 4.1 g
- Carbohydrates: 1.1 g

PREPARATION: 15 MIN **COOKING: 20 MIN** **SERVES: 2**

210. TROPICAL COCONUT BALLS

INGREDIENTS

- 1 cup shredded coconut (unsweetened)
- 6 tablespoons coconut milk (full-fat)
- 2 tablespoons melted coconut oil
- 1/4 cup almond flour
- 2 tablespoons lemon juice
- 2 tablespoons ground chia seeds
- Zest of 1 lemon
- 10 drops stevia (alcohol-free)
- 1/8 teaspoons sea salt

DIRECTIONS

1. Preheat the oven to 250°Fahrenheit
2. Place the shredded coconut in a large bowl and pour the coconut milk into it.
3. Add the almond flour, ground chia, sea salt, coconut oil, and lemon zest, and lemon juice to the bowl.
4. Mix everything until well combined.
5. Take 1 tablespoon of the mixture and form a ball out of it. Repeat with the remaining mixture.
6. Line a baking tray using parchment paper and place the small balls on it.
7. If you find the mixture too dry while making the balls, add one tablespoon (extra) of coconut oil to the mixture
8. Bake the coconut balls for 30 minutes and remove them from the oven.
9. Let it cool completely at room temperature.
10. Transfer the balls into another container carefully and refrigerate it for 30 minutes.
11. Serve chilled and enjoy!

NUTRITION

- Calories: 134
- Fat: 13.1 g
- Protein: 2.2 g
- Net Carb: 1.1 g

PREPARATION: 10 MIN **COOKING: 10 MIN** **SERVES: 6**

211. CHIA PEANUT BUTTER BITES

INGREDIENTS

- ½ ounce raw almonds
- 1 tablespoon powdered erythritol
- 4 teaspoons coconut oil
- 2 tablespoons canned coconut milk
- ½ teaspoon vanilla extract
- 2 tablespoons chia seeds, ground to powder
- ¼ cup coconut cream

DIRECTIONS

1. Put the almonds in a skillet over medium-low heat, and cook until toasted. Takes about 5 minutes.
2. Transfer the almonds to a food processor with the erythritol and 1 teaspoon coconut oil.
3. Blend until it forms a smooth almond butter.
4. Heat the rest of the coconut oil in a skillet over medium heat.
5. Add the coconut milk and vanilla and bring to a simmer.
6. Stir in the ground chia seeds, coconut cream, and almond butter.
7. Cook for 2 minutes, then spread in a foil-lined square dish.
8. Chill until the mixture is firm, then cut into squares to serve.

NUTRITION

- Calories: 110
- Fat: 8g
- Protein: 2g
- Net Carbs: 7g

PREPARATION: 10 MIN

COOKING: 15 MIN

SERVES: 6

212. ALMOND SESAME CRACKERS

INGREDIENTS

- 1 ½ cups almond flour
- ½ cup sesame seeds
- 1 teaspoon dried oregano
- ½ teaspoon salt
- 1 large egg, whisked
- 1 tablespoon coconut oil, melted

DIRECTIONS

1. Preheat the oven to 350°F
2. Whisk together the almond flour, sesame seeds, oregano, and salt in a bowl.
3. Add the eggs and coconut oil, stirring into a soft dough.
4. Sandwich the dough between two sheets of parchment and roll to 1/8" thickness.
5. Cut into squares and arrange them on the baking sheet.
6. Bake for 10 to 12 minutes or wait until browned around the edges.

NUTRITION

- Calories: 145
- Fat: 12.5g
- Protein: 5g
- Net Carbs: 2g

CONCLUSION

The ketogenic diet is the ultimate tool you can use to plan your future. Can you picture being more involved, more productive and efficient, and more relaxed and energetic? That future is possible for you, and it does not have to be a complicated process to achieve that vision. You can choose right now to be healthier and slimmer and more fulfilled tomorrow. It is possible with the ketogenic diet.

When people get older, their bones weaken. At 50, your bones at likely not as strong as they used to be. However, you can keep them in really good conditions. Consuming milk to give calcium cannot do enough to strengthen your bones. What you can do is to make use of the Keto diet as it is low in toxins. Toxins negatively affect the absorption of nutrients and so with this, your bones can take in all they need.

Whether you have met your weight loss goals, your life changes, or you simply want to eat whatever you want again. You cannot just suddenly start consuming carbs again for it will shock your system. Have an idea of what you want to allow back into your consumption slowly. Be familiar with portion sizes and stick to that amount of carbs for the first few times you eat post-keto.

Dealing with weight issues can be disheartening, and you do not have to be extremely overweight or obese to feel the effects. These extra pounds can put a strain on your overall health and wellness. They can make you less efficient in your work life and everyday activities. They can take you away from the things you like to do and the places you love to visit. They can make you feel winded and out of breath at the simplest activities. They can take away your joy for living and living life to the fullest.

The things to watch out for when coming off keto are weight gain, bloating, more energy, and feeling hungry. The weight gain is nothing to freak out over; perhaps, you might not even gain any. It all depends on your diet, how your body processes carbs, and, of course, water weight. The length of your keto diet is a significant factor in how much weight you have lost caused by the reduction of carbs. The bloating will occur because of the reintroduction of fibrous foods and your body getting used to digesting them again. The bloating van lasts for a few days to a few weeks. You will feel like you have more energy because carbs break down into glucose, which is the body's primary source of fuel. You may also notice better brain function and the ability to work out more.

Start with non-processed carbs like whole grain, beans, and fruits. Start slow and see how your body responds before resolving to add carbs one meal at a time.

This is not a fancy diet that promises falsehoods of miracle weight loss. This diet is proven by years of science and research, which benefits not only your waistline, but your heart, skin, brain, and organs. It does not just improve your physical health but your mental and emotional health as well. This diet improves your health holistically.

Made in the USA
Monee, IL
24 September 2021